FAITH LESSONS

ON THE

promised

LAND

CROSSROADS of THE WORLD

LEADER'S GUIDE

Also available from Ray Vander Laan

Video and Curriculum

Faith Lessons on the Death and Resurrection of the Messiah
Faith Lessons on the Life and Ministry of the Messiah
Faith Lessons on the Prophets and Kings of Israel

Book and Audiocassette

Echoes of His Presence

CD-ROM

Jesus: An Interactive Journey

FAITH LESSONS
ON THE
promised
LAND
CROSSROADS OF THE WORLD

LEADER'S GUIDE

Ray Vander Laan

with
Stephen and Amanda Sorenson

ZondervanPublishingHouse
Grand Rapids, Michigan

A Division of HarperCollinsPublishers

Faith Lessons on the Promised Land Leader's Guide

Copyright © 1999 by Ray Vander Laan

Requests for information should be addressed to:

ZondervanPublishingHouse
Grand Rapids, Michigan 49530

ISBN 0-310-67856-0

Interior design by Sherri Hoffman

Printed in the United States of America

00 01 02 03 04 /❖ CH/ 10 9 8 7 6 5 4 3 2

contents

Introduction

Because God speaks to us through the Scriptures, studying them is a rewarding experience. The inspired human authors of the Bible, as well as those to whom the words were originally given, were primarily Jews living in the Near East. God's words and actions spoke to them with such power, clarity, and purpose that they wrote them down and carefully preserved them as an authoritative body of literature.

God's use of human servants in revealing Himself resulted in writings that clearly bear the stamp of time and place. The message of the Scriptures is, of course, eternal and unchanging—but the circumstances and conditions of the people of the Bible are unique to their times. Consequently, we most clearly understand God's truth when we know the cultural context within which He spoke and acted and the perception of the people with whom He communicated. This does not mean that God's revelation is unclear if we don't know the cultural context. Rather, by learning how to think and approach life as Abraham, Moses, Ruth, Esther, and Paul did, modern Christians will deepen their appreciation of God's Word. To fully apply the message of the Bible, we must enter the world of the Hebrews and familiarize ourselves with their culture.

That is the purpose of this study. The events and characters of the Bible are presented in their original settings. Although the videos offer the latest archaeological research, this series is not intended to be a definitive cultural and geographical study of the lands of the Bible. No original scientific discoveries are revealed here. The purpose of this study is to help us better understand God's revealed mission for our lives by enabling us to hear and see His words in their original context.

understanding the world of the hebrews

More than 3,800 years ago, God spoke to His servant Abraham: "Go, walk through the length and breadth of the land, for I am giving it to you" (Genesis 13:17). From the outset, God's choice of a Hebrew nomad to begin His plan of salvation (that is still unfolding) was linked to the selection of a specific land where His redemptive work would begin. The nature of God's covenant relationship with His people demanded a place where their faith could be exercised and displayed to all nations so that the world would know of *Yahweh*, the true and faithful God. God showed the same care in preparing a land for His chosen people as He did in preparing a people to live in that land. For us to fully understand God's plan and purpose for His people, we must first understand the nature of the place He selected for them.

By New Testament times, the Jewish people had been removed from the Promised Land by the Babylonians due to Israel's failure to live obediently before God (Jeremiah 25:4–11). The exile lasted seventy years, but its impact upon God's people was astounding. New patterns of worship developed, and scribes and experts in God's law shaped the new commitment to be faithful to Him. The prophets predicted the appearance of a Messiah like King David who would revive the kingdom of the Hebrew people.

But the Promised Land was now home to many other groups of people whose religious practices, moral values, and lifestyles conflicted with those of the Jews. Living as God's witnesses took on added difficulty as Greek, Roman, and Samaritan worldviews mingled with that of the Israelites. The Promised Land was divided between kings and governors, usually under the authority of one foreign empire or another. But the mission of God's people did not change. They were still to live *so that the world would know that their God was the true God.* And the land continued to provide them opportunity to encounter the world that desperately needed to know this reality.

The Promised Land was the arena within which God's people were to serve Him faithfully as the world watched. The land God chose for His people was on the crossroads of the world. A major trade route, the Via Maris, ran through it. God intended for the Israelites to take control of the cities along this route and thereby exert influence on the nations around them. Through their righteous living, the Hebrews were to reveal the one true God, *Yahweh,* to the world. They failed to accomplish this mission, however, because of their unfaithfulness.

Western Christianity tends to spiritualize the concept of the Promised Land as it is presented in the Bible. Instead of seeing it as a crossroads from which to influence the world, modern Christians view it as a distant, heavenly city, a glorious "Canaan" toward which we are traveling as we ignore the world around us. We are focused on the destination, not the journey. We have unconsciously separated our walk with God from our responsibility to the world in which He has placed us. In one sense, our earthly experience is simply preparation for an eternity in the "promised land." Preoccupation with this idea, however, distorts the mission God has set for us.

Living by faith is not a vague, otherworldly experience; rather, it is being faithful to God right now, in the place and time in which He has put us. This truth is emphasized by God's choice of Canaan, a crossroads of the ancient world, as the Promised Land for the Israelites. God wants His people to be in the game, not on the bench. Our mission, as Christians today, is the same one He gave to the Israelites. We are to live obediently *within* the world so that through us *the world may know that our God is the one true God.*

The Assumptions of Biblical Writers

Biblical writers assumed that their readers were familiar with Near Eastern geography. The geography of Canaan shaped the culture of the people living there. Their settlements began near sources of water and food. Climate and raw materials shaped their choice of occupation, dress, weapons, diet, and even artistic expression. As their cities grew, they interacted politically. Trade developed, and trade routes were established.

During New Testament times, the Promised Land was called Palestine or Judea. *Judea* (which means "Jewish") technically referred to the land that had been the nation of Judah. Because of the influence that the people of Judea had over the rest of the land, the land itself was called Judea. The Romans divided the land into several provinces, including Judea, Samaria, and Galilee (the three main divisions during Jesus' time); Gaulanitis, the Decapolis, and Perea (east of the Jordan River); and Idumaea (Edom) and Nabatea (in the south). These further divisions of Israel added to the rich historical and cultural background God prepared for the coming of Jesus and the beginning of His church.

Today the names *Israel* and *Palestine* are often used to designate the land God gave to Abraham. Both terms are politically charged. *Palestine* is used by the Arabs living in the central part of the country, while *Israel* is used by the Jews to indicate the State of Israel. In this study, *Israel* is used in the biblical sense. This choice does not indicate a political statement regarding the current struggle in the Middle East but instead is chosen to best reflect the biblical designation for the land.

Unfortunately, many Christians do not have even a basic geographical knowledge of the region. This series is designed to help solve that problem. We will be studying the people and events of the Bible in their geographical and historical contexts. Once we know the *who*, *what*, and *where* of a Bible story, we will be able to understand the *why*. By deepening our understanding of God's Word, we can strengthen our relationship with God.

The biblical writers also used a language that, like all languages, is bound by culture and time. Therefore, understanding the Scriptures involves more than knowing what the words mean. We need to also understand those words from the perspective of the people who used them.

The people whom God chose as His instruments—the people to whom He revealed Himself—were Hebrews living in the Near East. These people described their world and themselves in concrete terms. Their language was one of pictures, metaphors, and examples rather than ideas, definitions, and abstractions. Whereas we might describe God as omniscient or omnipresent (knowing everything and present everywhere), a Hebrew would have preferred to describe God by saying, "The Lord is my shepherd." Thus, the Bible is filled with concrete images from Hebrew culture: God is our Father, and we are His children; God is the potter, and we are the clay; Jesus is the Lamb killed on Passover; Heaven is an oasis in the desert; and hell is the city sewage dump; the Last Judgment will be in the Eastern Gate of the heavenly Jerusalem and will include sheep and goats.

These people had an Eastern mindset rather than a Western mindset. Eastern thought emphasizes the process of learning as much or more than the end result. Whereas Westerners tend to collect information to find the right answer, Hebrew thought stresses the process of discovery as well as the answer. Thus in the Leader's Guide we have included *suggested responses* to the questions. These are provided primarily to help the leader determine the area(s) on which the participants should focus in discovering the answer(s). These suggested responses are not intended to be the final answers or provide an exhaustive list of possible responses. So, the effective leader will allow the participants to process the information and will stress the learning value of that process.

How to use this guide

This Leader's Guide is divided into five sessions approximately 50–55 minutes in length. Each session corresponds to a videotaped presentation by Ray Vander Laan.

For each session, *the leader* will need:

- Leader's Guide
- Bible
- Video player, monitor, stand, extension cord, etc.
- Videotape

Note: For some sessions, the leader may also want to use an overhead projector, chalk board, or marker board.

For each session, *the participant* will need:

- Participant's Guide
- Bible
- Pen or pencil

Directions to the leader are enclosed in the shaded boxes and are not meant to be spoken.

Each session is divided into six main parts: **Before You Lead, Introduction, Video Presentation, Group Discovery, Faith Lesson,** and **Closing Prayer**. A brief explanation of each part follows.

I. Before You Lead

Synopsis

This material is presented for the leader's information. It summarizes the material presented in each of the videos.

Key Points of This Lesson

Highlights the key points you'll want to emphasize.

Session Outline

Provides an overview of the content and activities to be covered throughout the session.

Materials

The materials listed above are critical for both the leader and each participant. Additional materials (optional) are listed when appropriate.

2. Introduction

Welcome

Welcomes participants to the session.

What's to Come

A brief summary you may choose to use as you begin the session.

Questions to Think About

Designed to help everyone begin thinking about the theme or topics that will be covered. A corresponding page is included in the Participant's Guide.

3. Video Presentation

This is the time during which you and the participants will watch the video and write down appropriate notes. Key themes have been indicated.

4. Group Discovery

In this section, you'll guide participants in thinking through materials and themes related to the video you've just seen. You may want to read the material word for word, or simply highlight key words and phrases. Feel free to amplify various points with your own material or illustrations.

The Leader's Guide includes a copy of the corresponding pages in the Participant's Guide. Space is also provided in which to write additional planning notes. Having the Participant's Guide pages in front of you allows you to view the pages the participants are seeing as you talk without having to hold two books at the same time. It also lets you know where the participants are in their book when someone asks you a question.

Video Highlights

Use these questions and suggested responses with the entire group. This will guide participants in verbally responding to key points/themes covered in the video.

Small Group Bible Discovery

At this time, if your group has more than seven participants you will break the group into small groups (three to five people) and assign each group a topic. (If you have more groups than topics, assign some topics to more than one group.) Participants will use their Bibles and write down suggested responses to the questions. At the end of this discovery time, participants will reassemble as a large group. As time allows, small group representatives can share key ideas their groups discussed.

Quite often supplementary material—called *Data File, Profile*, etc.—has been inserted near the topics. This material complements the themes but is not required reading to complete the session. Suggest that the participants read and study the supplementary material on their own.

5. faith lesson

Time for Reflection

At this time, participants will read selected Scripture passages on their own and think about questions that encourage them to apply what they've just discovered to their own lives.

Action Points

At this time, you'll summarize key points (provided for you) with the entire group and encourage participants to act on what they have learned.

6. closing prayer

Close the session with the material or prayer provided.

Before the first session

- Watch the video session.
- Obtain the necessary Participant's Guides for all participants
- Make sure you have the necessary equipment.

Tips for Leading and Promoting Group Discussion

1. Allow group members to participate at their own comfort level. Everyone need not answer every question.
2. Ask questions with interest and warmth and then listen carefully to individual responses. Remember: it is important for participants to think through the questions and ideas presented. The *process* is more important than specific *answers*, which is why *suggested responses* are provided.
3. Be flexible. Reword questions if necessary. Choose to spend more time on a topic. Add or delete questions to accommodate the needs of your group members—and your time frame.
4. Suggest that participants, during the coming week, do the Small Group Bible Discovery topics that their individual small groups may not have had the opportunity to do.
5. Allow for (and expect) differences of opinion and experience.
6. Gently guide all participants into discussion. Do not allow any person(s) to monopolize discussion.
7. Should a heated discussion begin on a theological topic, suggest that the participants involved continue their discussion after the session is over.
8. Do not be afraid of silence. Allow people time to think—don't panic. Sometimes ten seconds of silence seems like an eternity. Remember, some of this material requires time to process—so allow people time to digest a question and *then* respond.

standing at the crossroads

Before You Lead

Synopsis

The people who lived in the ancient land of Israel left behind an indelible record of their lives. An important part of that record lies in the mounds we call *tels*—piles of debris of ancient cities layered on top of one another—that contain evidence of the culture, architecture, art, diet, weapons, and even the writings of the people who lived there. As archaeologists peel away the layers of history preserved in these tels, the culture and people of the Bible come to light.

This video focuses on Tel Gezer, one of the greatest tels in Israel. To stand on this huge mound of ancient remains is to stand on a part of history that existed as many as 3,000 years before Christ. To the west of the ancient city of Gezer is the fertile coastal plain that lies along the Mediterranean Sea. To the east are the foothills—the *Shephelah*—beyond which lie the mountains of Judea and beyond them the forbidding Arabian Desert. Jerusalem—the highest point in the hills of Judea—is only about fifteen miles from Gezer. Egypt, which was the technologically advanced world power of the time, lies to the southwest. To the east is Mesopotamia, the home of civilizations that the Bible refers to as Persia, Babylon, and Assyria.

Gezer was significant because it was located at the crossroads of the ancient world. It was next to the coastal road—the Via Maris—that ran between Egypt and Mesopotamia, two civilizations that needed each other for economic and cultural reasons. The key road running east and west toward Jericho also intersected the Via Maris at Gezer. So, rather than being a quiet, agricultural area, as people who view it today might imagine, Gezer was truly a city "in between." It bustled with commercial activity. Whoever controlled Gezer could, in effect, control world trade. Unfortunately, the Israelites failed to control this city (Joshua 16:10) and never exerted the kind of influence upon the world that God desired them to have.

In this video, Ray Vander Laan shares insights concerning the:

- Ruins of Gezer, including an area where archaeologists have uncovered a huge, six-chambered gate complex dating back to King Solomon's time (about 920 B.C.).
- Trench that ran under the main city street and carried sewage into the refuse heap in the valley below.
- Key functions that took place at the city gate.
- Significance of "standing stones"—the stone pillars that people in the Middle East erected where religiously or politically significant events occurred. They were memorials to great events that could only be explained as supernatural.

The most important concept of this lesson, however, is that God placed the children of Israel at the crossroads of the world. There He wanted His people to influence His world. There He wanted to create morality and justice. There He wanted to demonstrate salvation. But what happened? The Israelites chose to live in the mountains and allowed the Canaanites to live on the coastal plain and in the city of Gezer. Thus they gave the pagans the major influence over culture and the rest of the world.

Key Points of This Lesson

1. *God wants His people to greatly influence the culture of their world.* That is why He placed His people in the land of Israel and wanted them to occupy the city of Gezer, which was an international crossroads. Likewise, God wants you and me—His followers today—to live at the crossroads of life. He wants us to live so publicly that we become a "flavoring influence" on our culture. Rather than isolating ourselves from the world, God wants us to actively participate in and control areas that shape our culture and the world as a whole.

2. *Israel failed to conquer the Gezers of their world and as a result failed in their mission to be God's witnesses to the world.* We also fail in our mission as God's witnesses to the world when we don't take control and exert a godly influence on that which is significant in our culture.

3. *Just as the people of ancient Israel erected "standing stones" to commemorate God's supernatural actions on their behalf (such as when He gave them the Ten Commandments), God wants each of us to be a* massebah—*a living, standing stone.* In 1 Peter 2:4–5, we learn that we, "like living stones are being built into a spiritual house." Each of us is like a piece of stone that God is shaping and cutting in order to build His house—His world, His kingdom, His church. He wants us to exhibit Him to a watching world. As we live godly lives, non-Christians will see our good deeds and be drawn toward God—just as the people in ancient times were reminded about what God had done for them when they saw standing stones.

Session Outline (55 minutes)

I. Introduction (4 minutes)
Welcome
What's to Come
Questions to Think About

II. Show Video "Standing at the Crossroads" (22 minutes)

III. Group Discovery (20 minutes)
Video Highlights
Small Group Bible Discovery

IV. Faith Lesson (8 minutes)
Time for Reflection
Action Points

V. Closing Prayer (1 minute)

Materials

No additional materials are needed for this session. Simply view the video prior to leading the session so you are familiar with its main points.

standing at the crossroads

introduction

4 minutes

Welcome

> Assemble the participants together. Welcome them to session one of *Faith Lessons on the Promised Land*.

What's to Come

In this session, we'll view the ruins of Tel Gezer and learn why God placed the children of Israel at the crossroads of civilization. We'll also learn that God calls us, as Christians, to stand at the crossroads of our world. He calls us to actively participate in shaping our culture and our world. He calls us to live godly lives that will draw non-Christians toward Him.

Questions to Think About

> *Participant's Guide page 11.*

Before we begin the video, let's think about the crossroads in our lives. Several questions to consider are on page 11 of your Participant's Guide.

> Ask each question and solicit a few responses from group members.

✏ 1.   Think for a moment about where you live, what you do, and the people with whom you have contact. Can you think of specific reasons why God might have placed you where you are?

Suggested Responses: Allow participants to share their ideas. Perhaps they believe they have a specific task to accomplish, there is a specific person they believe they are to witness to, or they don't know why they are where they are.

✏ 2.   Remember when you have faced a difficult decision or resolved a crisis at a key crossroads in your life. Now imagine that another person is facing a similar challenge. If you had had the opportunity, what might you have left behind that would help that person benefit from your experience?

Suggested Responses: a journal, videotape, photographs, list of pros and cons, a legacy of changed lives, a lasting impact on society, etc.

SESSION ONE

standing at the crossroads

questions to think about

1. Think for a moment about where you live, what you do, and the people with whom you have contact. Can you think of specific reasons why God might have placed you where you are?

2. Remember when you have faced a difficult decision or resolved a crisis at a key crossroads in your life. Now imagine that another person is facing a similar challenge. If you had had the opportunity, what might you have left behind that would help that person benefit from your experience?

3. In what ways can we as Christians exert more influence on our culture and help people discover God?

11

PLANNING NOTES:

✏ 3.   In what ways can we as Christians exert more influence on our culture and help people discover God?

Suggested Responses: live more godly lives, become involved in community decisions, run for local political offices, assume key positions in corporate America, become active in volunteer work, make more of an effort to reach out to non-Christians in our neighborhoods and communities, etc.

Let's keep these ideas in mind as we view the video.

video presentation

22 minutes

| Participant's Guide page 12. |

On page 12 of your Participant's Guide, you will find a space in which to take notes on key points as we watch this video.

Leader's Video Observations

Tel Gezer: Crossroads of the World

City Gates

Standing Stones

SESSION ONE

standing at the crossroads

questions to think about

1. Think for a moment about where you live, what you do, and the people with whom you have contact. Can you think of specific reasons why God might have placed you where you are?

2. Remember when you have faced a difficult decision or resolved a crisis at a key crossroads in your life. Now imagine that another person is facing a similar challenge. If you had had the opportunity, what might you have left behind that would help that person benefit from your experience?

3. In what ways can we as Christians exert more influence on our culture and help people discover God?

11

---

12   Faith Lessons on the Promised Land

video notes

Tel Gezer: Crossroads of the World

City Gates

Standing Stones

Group Discovery

20 minutes

If your group has seven or more members, use the **Video Highlights** with the entire group (5 minutes), then break into small groups of three to five to discuss the **Small Group Bible Discovery** (10 minutes). Then reassemble the group to discuss the key points discovered (5 minutes).

If your group has fewer than seven members, begin with the **Video Highlights** (5 minutes), then do one or more of the topics found in the **Small Group Bible Discovery** as a group (10 minutes). Finally, spend five minutes at the end discussing points that had an impact on participants.

Video Highlights (5 minutes)

Here you'll ask one or more of the following questions that directly relate to the video the participants have just seen.

Look at the map of Israel on page 13 of your Participant's Guide and locate Gezer.

Israel

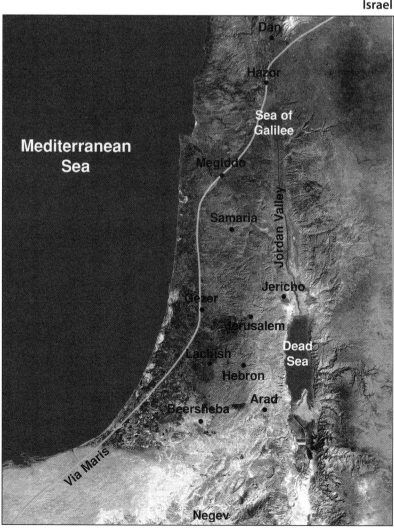

video highlights

Look at the map of Israel below and locate Gezer.

1. What is so significant about Tel Gezer's location?

✎ 1.   What is so significant about Tel Gezer's location?

Suggested Responses: Gezer was located along the Via Maris, the key north-south coastal road, and along the east-west road to Jericho. Its location along the main trade route linking Egypt and Mesopotamia positioned it at the crossroads of the Middle Eastern world, etc.

✎ 2.   What did God intend to accomplish by choosing the land of Israel as the place where His people would live? What did the Israelites do that diminished the effectiveness of God's plan?

Suggested Response: God wanted His people to live as His witnesses to the world. He wanted their lives to be a testimony of who He is. Instead of living in their God-given position of influence and making an impact for God among the ancient civilizations of that day, the Israelites chose to live in the mountains and allowed the Canaanites to live in influential places.

✎ 3.   What new information or insight about city gates did you gain from the video?

Suggested Responses: how large the gates were—perhaps twenty feet high; that the gates opened into a large room surrounded by additional rooms; that so much judicial, political, and financial business was conducted at the city gate; etc.

✎ 4.   What are "standing stones," and why were they erected?

Suggested Response: Standing stones are large stones that have been placed into the ground pointing upward. Middle Eastern people erected standing stones to commemorate significant religious and political events, so that people who passed by the stones would wonder and/or be reminded of what had happened there.

THE TRUTH OF THE MATTER

Even though the Israelites seldom inhabited Gezer, and thus allowed the Canaanites to wield a much greater influence on the world's culture than they otherwise would have, the Canaanites living there did not have an easy life. In fact, the people of Gezer had a rough life. Consider:

- When Joshua led the Israelites into Canaan, Horam—the king of Gezer—attacked them, but Horam and his troops were all killed (Joshua 10:33).
- The tribe of Ephraim allowed the Canaanites to continue living in Gezer, but they used them as forced labor (Joshua 16:10).
- Pharaoh, king of Egypt, attacked and captured Gezer and then set it on fire. He killed its Canaanite inhabitants and gave it as a wedding gift to his daughter, Solomon's wife (1 Kings 9:16).
- During King David's reign, the Israelites battled the Philistines at Gezer (1 Chronicles 20:4). Years later, Solomon rebuilt Gezer's walls (including its huge, six-chambered gate) using forced laborers (1 Kings 9:15–17a).

2. What did God intend to accomplish by choosing the land of Israel as the place where His people would live? What did the Israelites do that diminished the effectiveness of God's plan?

3. What new information or insight about city gates did you gain from the video?

4. What are "standing stones," and why were they erected?

THE TRUTH OF THE MATTER

Even though the Israelites seldom inhabited Gezer, and thus allowed the Canaanites to wield a much greater influence on the world's culture than they otherwise would have, the Canaanites living there did not have an easy life. In fact, the people of Gezer had a rough life. Consider:

- When Joshua led the Israelites into Canaan, Horam—the king of Gezer—attacked them, but Horam and his troops were all killed (Joshua 10:33).
- The tribe of Ephraim allowed the Canaanites to continue living in Gezer, but they used them as forced labor (Joshua 16:10).
- Pharaoh, king of Egypt, attacked and captured Gezer and then set it on fire. He killed its Canaanite inhabitants and gave it as a wedding gift to his daughter, Solomon's wife (1 Kings 9:16).
- During King David's reign, the Israelites battled the Philistines at Gezer (1 Chronicles 20:4). Years later, Solomon rebuilt Gezer's walls (including its huge, six-chambered gate) using forced laborers (1 Kings 9:15–17a).

PLANNING NOTES:

Small Group Bible Discovery (10 minutes)

> *Participant's Guide pages 16–23.*
>
> During this time, a group with fewer than seven participants will stay together. A group larger than seven participants will break into small groups and reassemble as a large group during the final five minutes. Assign each group one of the following topics. If you have more than four small groups, assign some topics to more than one group.

Let's break into groups of three to five—people sitting near you—and study some of the Bible passages and truths mentioned in the video.

Turn to pages 16–23 in your Participant's Guide. There you'll find a list of four topics. You'll have ten minutes to read and discuss the topic I'll assign to you. Choose one person in your group to be a spokesperson for your group when we discuss these topics later.

> Assign each group a topic.

I'll signal you when one minute is left.

> After nine minutes, let participants know that they have one minute remaining. Then reassemble the entire group. After everyone is back together, begin asking one person from each small group to briefly share a key idea with the larger group. In some cases, you may not have time for every group to share their discoveries.

As time allows, let's briefly share the key ideas that your group discussed.

Topic A: God Carries Out His Plans

The Bible, especially the Old Testament, teaches that God is "sovereign"—in absolute control of all things. He has the power and patience to carry out through human history everything He has planned and promised to do.

1. Who did God choose to be the founder of Israel, and what did God promise to do? (See Genesis 12:1–3.)

    Suggested Responses: God chose Abram (later named Abraham) to be the founder of a people who would reside in a special land God had prepared for them. God then promised to make Abram's lineage into a great nation, to bless Abram, to make his name great, to use him to bless other people, to bless people who bless him, to curse people who curse him, and to bless everyone on earth through him. [Note: be sure to emphasize that God had selected the land—to put His people at the crossroads of ancient civilization. The place God chose was just as important as His people and His plan.]

small Group Bible Discovery

Topic A: God Carries Out His Plans

The Bible, especially the Old Testament, teaches that God is "sovereign"—in absolute control of all things. He has the power and patience to carry out through human history everything He has planned and promised to do.

1. Who did God choose to be the founder of Israel, and what did God promise to do? (See Genesis 12:1–3.)

2. What plot did Haman plan for the Jews, and how did God plan to use Esther—the Jewish queen of the King of Persia? (See Esther 3:1–6, 13; 4:1, 5–14.)

3. At times, God's plans seem doomed to failure. One such instance was during King Hezekiah's reign when King Sennacherib of Assyria threatened to destroy Jerusalem. Read Isaiah 37:15–22, 26, 32–36. In light of God's plan to make Himself known to the world, which significant truths are revealed in the following verses?

16	
17	
18–19	
20	

PLANNING NOTES:

2. What plot did Haman plan for the Jews, and how did God plan to use Esther—the Jewish queen of the King of Persia? (See Esther 3:1–6, 13; 4:1, 5–14.)

Suggested Responses: Haman—an honored Persian noble—became enraged at Mordecai—a Jew who wouldn't bow down to him. So Haman plotted to kill all the Jews. God, in turn, planned to use Esther to save His people.

3. At times, God's plans seem doomed to failure. One such instance was during King Hezekiah's reign when King Sennacherib of Assyria threatened to destroy Jerusalem. Read Isaiah 37:15–22, 26, 32–36. In light of God's plan to make Himself known to the world, which significant truths are revealed in the following verses?

16	Hezekiah affirmed who God is
17	Sennacherib reproached God
18–19	The situation was hopeless; the destruction of Jerusalem was certain
20	Hezekiah asked for deliverance so that the world would know that God alone is God
26	God had planned it all long ago and was bringing His plan to pass
32–34	God Himself would act to ensure that a remnant of His people would survive
35	God would save the city for His sake and for David's sake

4. What does Galatians 4:4–5 reveal about God's plan of salvation?

Suggested Response: When the time was right, God sent Jesus, His Son, into the world to redeem people from their sins.

Topic B: God's Plan for His People

1. What did God, speaking through the prophet Isaiah, say that His people were to be? (See Isaiah 43:10–13.)

Suggested Responses: witnesses and servants to the truth that He alone is God and savior.

2. What, according to Solomon, was the reason God's people were to obey Him? (See 1 Kings 8:56–60.)

Suggested Response: so that all people would know that "the Lord is God and that there is no other."

small Group Bible Discovery

Topic A: God Carries Out His Plans

The Bible, especially the Old Testament, teaches that God is "sovereign"—in absolute control of all things. He has the power and patience to carry out through human history everything He has planned and promised to do.

1. Who did God choose to be the founder of Israel, and what did God promise to do? (See Genesis 12:1–3.)

2. What plot did Haman plan for the Jews, and how did God plan to use Esther—the Jewish queen of the King of Persia? (See Esther 3:1–6, 13; 4:1, 5–14.)

3. At times, God's plans seem doomed to failure. One such instance was during King Hezekiah's reign when King Sennacherib of Assyria threatened to destroy Jerusalem. Read Isaiah 37:15–22, 26, 32–36. In light of God's plan to make Himself known to the world, which significant truths are revealed in the following verses?

16	
17	
18–19	
20	

26	
32–34	
35	

4. What does Galatians 4:4–5 reveal about God's plan of salvation?

Topic B: God's Plan for His People

1. What did God, speaking through the prophet Isaiah, say that His people were to be? (See Isaiah 43:10–13.)

2. What, according to Solomon, was the reason God's people were to obey Him? (See 1 Kings 8:56–60.)

3. In each of the following Scriptures, what motivated the key person in the story?

Joshua 4:19–24	
1 Kings 18:21, 36–39	
Matthew 15:29–31	

3. In each of the following Scriptures, what motivated the key person in the story?

Joshua 4:19–24	Joshua sought to create a memorial to God so that all the people of the earth would know that the hand of God is powerful and to remind the Israelites to fear the Lord their God forever.
1 Kings 18:21, 36–39	Elijah wanted the people, who had been worshiping Baal, to know that the Lord was God and that He was turning their hearts back toward Him.
Matthew 15:29–31	When Jesus healed the people, they marveled and glorified the God of Israel.

4. What do the words of Rahab, the prostitute in Jericho who protected the spies of Israel, reveal about the effectiveness of God's plan when His people fulfill their part? (See Joshua 2:8–11.)

Suggested Responses: The people will know that God is God and will be fearful of what will happen to them if they are enemies of God.

Topic C: City Gates

During biblical times, the city gate protected the entrance to the city and also functioned as the "city hall." So rulers, judges, or other officials "sat in the gate."

City Gates

26	
32–34	
35	

4. What does Galatians 4:4–5 reveal about God's plan of salvation?

Topic B: God's Plan for His People

1. What did God, speaking through the prophet Isaiah, say that His people were to be? (See Isaiah 43:10–13.)

2. What, according to Solomon, was the reason God's people were to obey Him? (See 1 Kings 8:56–60.)

3. In each of the following Scriptures, what motivated the key person in the story?

Joshua 4:19–24	
1 Kings 18:21, 36–39	
Matthew 15:29–31	

4. What do the words of Rahab, the prostitute in Jericho who protected the spies of Israel, reveal about the effectiveness of God's plan when His people fulfill their part? (See Joshua 2:8–11.)

Topic C: City Gates

During biblical times, the city gate protected the entrance to the city and also functioned as the "city hall." So rulers, judges, or other officials "sat in the gate."

City Gates

✏ 1.   Look up each of the following Scriptures and note what you learn about the people and their function in relationship to the city gates.

   a. Genesis 13:10–13; 18:20–21; 19:1, 9

       Suggested Responses: Abraham and Lot parted company, and Lot went to live in Sodom. When God's angels arrived in Sodom, Lot was "in the gateway," apparently serving as an influential (and apparently not always appreciated) judge in that evil city.

   b. Deuteronomy 21:18–21

       Suggested Responses: Parents of a rebellious son who wouldn't submit to their discipline were to take him to the city gate and present him to the elders there. Then all the males in the city were to stone that son to death. Because the gate was at the center of community activities, word of what happened would spread quickly, and the people of Israel would be less likely to do evil.

   c. Ruth 4:1–11

       Suggested Responses: Boaz, a town leader, sat at the gate and asked ten town elders to sit with him. Then he presented Naomi's situation to a relative of hers, and the elders witnessed the final ruling. The gate was clearly a place where legal decisions were made and witnessed.

   d. 1 Samuel 4:10–18

       Suggested Responses: When a soldier arrived at Shiloh and told the town that the Philistines had captured the ark of the covenant, Eli was sitting in the gate. There, in that place of honor where he had judged the people for forty years, he fell off his chair, broke his neck, and died.

   e. 2 Samuel 18:1–5; 19:1–8

       Suggested Responses: King David stood by the gate and gave last-minute instructions when he sent his army out to fight against Absalom. When David ceased mourning Absalom's death, he returned to his place at the gate, and the people came to him.

   f. Esther 2:5–8, 19–23

       Suggested Responses: Mordecai, who had adopted Esther when her parents died, is described as "sitting at the king's gate." While there, he learned of a plot to assassinate the king. So he told Queen Esther, who in turn told the king. The fact that Mordecai was in the gate shows that he was a community leader.

Session One: Standing at the Crossroads   19

1. Look up each of the following Scriptures and note what
   you learn about the people and their function in relationship to the city gates.

   a. Genesis 13:10–13; 18:20–21; 19:1, 9

   b. Deuteronomy 21:18–21

   c. Ruth 4:1–11

   d. 1 Samuel 4:10–18

   e. 2 Samuel 18:1–5; 19:1–8

   f. Esther 2:5–8, 19–23

PLANNING NOTES:

DATA FILE

Solomon's Gate at Gezer

The Important Role of City Gates

During biblical times, city gates:

- Prevented enemies from entering the city through entry points in the city wall.
- Functioned as the center of city life—like a city hall or courthouse today. In various chambers inside the gatehouse, people paid their taxes, settled legal matters, and even met with the king. Soldiers were stationed there, too.
- Provided a gathering place for prophets, kings, priests, judges, and other city leaders. For example, Jehoshaphat (king of Judah) and Ahab (king of Israel) sat on their thrones in the gate of Samaria (1 Kings 22:10).

The Role of the Eastern Gate in the Life of the Messiah

The Bible predicts that the Messiah will enter the temple through the Eastern (or Beautiful) Gate. This prediction is taken so seriously by Islamic leaders that they have blocked the gate and built a cemetery in front of it in an effort to prevent the Messiah from entering the Temple Mount!

Not only will the Messiah enter the temple through the Eastern Gate, tradition says that it will be the symbolic or literal location of the Last Judgment. Consider these Scriptures:

- The Last Judgment will take place in the Jehoshaphat Valley, just east of Jerusalem (Joel 3:2, 12).
- The power of God will establish Jerusalem as the Heavenly City (Zechariah 14:1–11).
- After the Last Judgment, the saved will enter the gate of the Heavenly City (Isaiah 62:10, Revelation 21). Since the setting is on the east side of Jerusalem, the gate would be the Beautiful or Eastern Gate.

20   Faith Lessons on the Promised Land

DATA FILE
Solomon's Gate at Gezer

The Important Role of City Gates
During biblical times, city gates:

- Prevented enemies from entering the city through entry points in the city wall.
- Functioned as the center of city life—like a city hall or courthouse today. In various chambers inside the gatehouse, people paid their taxes, settled legal matters, and even met with the king. Soldiers were stationed there, too.
- Provided a gathering place for prophets, kings, priests, judges, and other city leaders. For example, Jehoshaphat (king of Judah) and Ahab (king of Israel) sat on their thrones in the gate of Samaria (1 Kings 22:10).

Session One: Standing at the Crossroads   21

The Role of the Eastern Gate in the Life of the Messiah
The Bible predicts that the Messiah will enter the temple through the Eastern (or Beautiful) Gate. This prediction is taken so seriously by Islamic leaders that they have blocked the gate and built a cemetery in front of it in an effort to prevent the Messiah from entering the Temple Mount!

Not only will the Messiah enter the temple through the Eastern Gate, tradition says that it will be the symbolic or literal location of the Last Judgment. Consider these Scriptures:

- The Last Judgment will take place in the Jehoshaphat Valley, just east of Jerusalem (Joel 3:2, 12).
- The power of God will establish Jerusalem as the Heavenly City (Zechariah 14:1–11).
- After the Last Judgment, the saved will enter the gate of the Heavenly City (Isaiah 62:10; Revelation 21). Since the setting is on the east side of Jerusalem, the gate would be the Beautiful or Eastern Gate.

Topic D: Standing Stones

God's work in the past—the distant past or in our own past—is the foundation on which our belief in God and commitment to Him are built. Recognizing the importance of remembering what God had done for them, God's people in the Bible erected standing stones as memorials to God's supernatural acts on their behalf. The Canaanites also erected standing stones to their gods.

1. What is the difference between the standing stones mentioned in Genesis 28:18–22 and those described in 1 Kings 14:22–23?

Topic D: Standing Stones

God's work in the past—the distant past or in our own past—is the foundation on which our belief in God and commitment to Him are built. Recognizing the importance of remembering what God had done for them, God's people in the Bible erected standing stones as memorials to God's supernatural acts on their behalf. The Canaanites also erected standing stones to their gods.

✏ 1. What is the difference between the standing stones mentioned in Genesis 28:18–22 and those described in 1 Kings 14:22–23?

Suggested Responses: The standing stone of Genesis 28:18 represented the presence of God and stood as a memorial to Jacob's commitment to God. The stones mentioned in 1 Kings 14:22–23 represented the people's devotion to idolatry and the fertility religions of the nations the Lord dispossessed for the nation of Israel.

✏ 2. Look up the following verses. What do they say about the pagan use of standing stones?

a. Leviticus 26:1

Suggested Response: God's people were not to erect standing stones for the purpose of worship.

b. Deuteronomy 16:21–22 and Exodus 23:24

Suggested Response: God hated sacred stones erected for idol worship and commanded the Israelites to break them.

✏ 3. For each of the following passages, summarize the story or event and note the work of God that the standing stones commemorate or represent.

a. Genesis 35:1–3, 14–15

Suggested Responses: After Jacob left the pagan world of his father-in-law, he returned to Bethel where God had spoken to him years before. Next to the original standing stone Jacob had left years earlier, God spoke to Jacob again, and Jacob erected a second stone pillar as a monument to the presence and power of God.

b. Exodus 24:1–5

Suggested Responses: On Mt. Sinai, God told Moses the laws the Israelites were to obey, and established a covenant with them. In response, Moses built an altar to God at the foot of Mt. Sinai and erected twelve stone pillars that represented the twelve tribes of Israel. These "standing stones" were a testimony to God's covenant with Israel.

c. Joshua 3:14–17; 4:4–9

Suggested Responses: God miraculously held back the water of the Jordan River so that the Israelites could cross near Jericho. So, the people set up twelve stones removed from the dry riverbed and erected them at the spot where they camped after crossing the river. There, the stones were a memorial to the children of Israel.

The Role of the Eastern Gate in the Life of the Messiah
The Bible predicts that the Messiah will enter the temple through the Eastern (or Beautiful) Gate. This prediction is taken so seriously by Islamic leaders that they have blocked the gate and built a cemetery in front of it in an effort to prevent the Messiah from entering the Temple Mount!

Not only will the Messiah enter the temple through the Eastern Gate, tradition says that it will be the symbolic or literal location of the Last Judgment. Consider these Scriptures:

- The Last Judgment will take place in the Jehoshaphat Valley, just east of Jerusalem (Joel 3:2, 12).
- The power of God will establish Jerusalem as the Heavenly City (Zechariah 14:1–11).
- After the Last Judgment, the saved will enter the gate of the Heavenly City (Isaiah 62:10; Revelation 21). Since the setting is on the east side of Jerusalem, the gate would be the Beautiful or Eastern Gate.

Topic D: Standing Stones

God's work in the past—the distant past or in our own past—is the foundation on which our belief in God and commitment to Him are built. Recognizing the importance of remembering what God had done for them, God's people in the Bible erected standing stones as memorials to God's supernatural acts on their behalf. The Canaanites also erected standing stones to their gods.

1. What is the difference between the standing stones mentioned in Genesis 28:18–22 and those described in 1 Kings 14:22–23?

2. Look up the following verses. What do they say about the pagan use of standing stones?

   a. Leviticus 26:1

   b. Deuteronomy 16:21–22 and Exodus 23:24

3. For each of the following passages, summarize the story or event and note the work of God that the standing stones commemorate or represent.

   a. Genesis 35:1–3, 14–15

   b. Exodus 24:1–5

   c. Joshua 3:14–17; 4:4–9

   d. Joshua 24:19–27

PLANNING NOTES:

    d. Joshua 24:19–27

Suggested Responses: Joshua challenged the people to decide whether or not they would serve the Lord. They agreed to serve and obey Him, so Joshua drew up decrees and laws for them to follow. Then Joshua set up a standing stone, to remind the people of God's words and their commitment to Him.

✏ 4.   Read 1 Peter 2:4–12. In what ways is a believer like a living stone?

Suggested Responses: A believer is a living stone being built into the spiritual "house" of God. In verse 12, God encourages believers to "live such good lives among the pagans that ... they may see your good deeds and glorify God." Like the standing stones that represented the work of God in a particular place or in the life of a person and so pointed people to God, followers of Jesus must live so that the world will know that the Lord is God.

DATA FILE

At the high place at Gezer, ten stones (some more than twenty feet tall) stand in silent tribute to a now forgotten event. Lonely sentinels on the ruins of ancient cities, these gigantic standing stones provide a glimpse into a custom popular thousands of years ago. Any travelers who saw the stones would know that something significant had happened there.

Long before the Israelites entered Canaan, pagans in the Middle East erected sacred stones to their gods, to declare covenants and treaties between cities or individuals, and to honor gods they believed caused an important event or provided a significant benefit.

The Hebrew word translated "standing stones" is *massebah* and means "to set up." Perhaps our practice of placing tombstones over the graves of loved ones is derived from a special standing stone called a *stele* (plural: *stelae*). These stones were erected as *masseboth* (standing stones) but had stories or inscriptions carved on them explaining their significance.

Archaeologists in the Middle East have unearthed many *stelae*, including one found in 1993 at Tel Dan that mentions the name "David"—the only extrabiblical reference to David ever discovered. To date, no *massebah* or *stele* specifically mentioned in the Bible has been found.

4. Read 1 Peter 2:4–12. In what ways is a believer like a living stone?

DATA FILE

At the high place at Gezer, ten stones (some more than twenty feet tall) stand in silent tribute to a now-forgotten event. Lonely sentinels on the ruins of ancient cities, these gigantic standing stones provide a glimpse into a custom popular thousands of years ago. Any travelers who saw the stones would know that something significant had happened there.

Long before the Israelites entered Canaan, pagans in the Middle East erected sacred stones to their gods, to declare covenants and treaties between cities or individuals, and to honor gods they believed caused an important event or provided a significant benefit.

The Hebrew word translated "standing stones" is *massebah* and means "to set up." Perhaps our practice of placing tombstones over the graves of loved ones is derived from a special standing stone called a *stele* (plural: *stelae*). These stones were erected as *masseboth* (standing stones) but had stories or inscriptions carved on them explaining their significance.

Archaeologists in the Middle East have unearthed many *stelae*, including one found in 1993 at Tel Dan that mentions the name "David" — the only extrabiblical reference to David ever discovered. To date, no *massebah* or *stele* specifically mentioned in the Bible has been found.

faith Lesson

8 minutes

Time for Reflection (4 minutes)

It's time for each of us to think quietly about how we live our lives before a watching world. On page 24 of the Participant's Guide, you'll find a passage of Scripture. Let's each read this passage silently and take the next few minutes to consider some of the questions that follow the Scripture passage.

Please do not talk during this time. It's a time when we all can reflect on today's lesson and how it applies to our lives.

The Scripture passage and questions are reproduced in their entirety in the Participant's Guide pages 24–25.

Goliath stood and shouted to the ranks of Israel, "Why do you come out and line up for battle? Am I not a Philistine, and are you not the servants of Saul? Choose a man and have him come down to me. If he is able to fight and kill me, we will become your subjects; but if I overcome him and kill him, you will become our subjects and serve us."

Then the Philistine said, "This day I defy the ranks of Israel! Give me a man and let us fight each other."

On hearing the Philistine's words, Saul and all the Israelites were dismayed and terrified. . . .

David said to Saul, "Let no one lose heart on account of this Philistine; your servant will go and fight him. . . .

"Your servant has killed both the lion and the bear; this uncircumcised Philistine will be like one of them, because he has defied the armies of the living God. The LORD who delivered me from the paw of the lion and the paw of the bear will deliver me from the hand of this Philistine."

Saul said to David, "Go, and the LORD be with you." . . .

David said to the Philistine, "You come against me with sword and spear and javelin, but I come against you in the name of the LORD Almighty, the God of the armies of Israel, whom you have defied. This day the LORD will hand you over to me, and I'll strike you down and cut off your head. Today I will give the carcasses of the Philistine army to the birds of the air and the beasts of the earth, and the whole world will know that there is a God in Israel. All those gathered here will know that it is not by sword or spear that the LORD saves; for the battle is the LORD's, and he will give all of you into our hands."

1 SAMUEL 17:8–11, 32, 36–37, 45–47

1. David clearly recognized that he stood at a crossroads and that he had a role to play in making the God of Israel known to the world. In what ways do you stand at a crossroads?

2. What could *you* do to publicly exert godly influence within your sphere of influence? In what arenas would God have you act to show that He is the Lord God?

faith Lesson

Time for Reflection

Read the following passage of Scripture and take the next few minutes to reflect on today's lesson and how it applies to your life.

Goliath stood and shouted to the ranks of Israel, "Why do you come out and line up for battle? Am I not a Philistine, and are you not the servants of Saul? Choose a man and have him come down to me. If he is able to fight and kill me, we will become your subjects; but if I overcome him and kill him, you will become our subjects and serve us."

Then the Philistine said, "This day I defy the ranks of Israel! Give me a man and let us fight each other."

On hearing the Philistine's words, Saul and all the Israelites were dismayed and terrified. . . .

David said to Saul, "Let no one lose heart on account of this Philistine; your servant will go and fight him. . . .

"Your servant has killed both the lion and the bear; this uncircumcised Philistine will be like one of them, because he has defied the armies of the living God. The Lord who delivered me from the paw of the lion and the paw of the bear will deliver me from the hand of this Philistine."

Saul said to David, "Go, and the Lord be with you." . . .

David said to the Philistine, "You come against me with sword and spear and javelin, but I come against you in the name of the Lord Almighty, the God of the armies of Israel, whom you have defied. This day the Lord will hand you over to me, and I'll strike you down and cut off your head. Today I will give the carcasses of the Philistine army to the birds of the air and the beasts of the earth, and the whole world will know that there is a God in Israel. All those gathered here will know that it is not by sword or spear that the Lord saves; for the battle is the Lord's, and he will give all of you into our hands."

1 Samuel 17:8–11, 32, 36–37, 45–47

1. David clearly recognized that he stood at a crossroads and that he had a role to play in making the God of Israel known to the world. In what ways do you stand at a crossroads?

2. What could *you* do to publicly exert godly influence within your sphere of influence? In what arenas would God have you act to show that He is the Lord God?

3. How does God's call for you to exhibit Him in all that you do, think, and say affect what you do every day?

Action Points

Take a moment to review the key points you explored today. Then write down an action step (or steps) that you will commit to this week as a result of what you have learned.

1. *God wants His people to greatly influence the culture of their world.* That is why He placed His people in the land of Israel and wanted them to occupy the city of Gezer, which was an international crossroads.

   Likewise, God wants you and me—His followers today—to live at the crossroads of life. He wants us to live so publicly that we become a "flavoring influence" on our culture. Rather than isolating ourselves from the world, God wants us to actively participate in and control areas that shape our culture and the world as a whole.

   The crossroads at which I believe God wants me to make an impact is: _____

PLANNING NOTES:

✏ 3.   How does God's call for you to exhibit Him in all that you do, think, and say affect what you do every day?

> As soon as participants have spent four minutes reflecting on the above questions, get the entire group's attention and move to the next section.

Action Points (4 minutes)

> *The following points are reproduced on pages 25–26 of the Participant's Guide:*

Now it's time to wrap up our session.

> Give participants a moment to transition from their thoughtfulness to giving you their full attention.

I'd like to take a moment to summarize the key points we explored. After I have reviewed each point, I will pause for a moment so that you may jot down an action step (or steps) that you will commit to this week as a result of what you have learned today.

> Read each point and pause after each point so that participants can consider and write out their commitment.

✏ 1.   *God wants His people to greatly influence the culture of their world.* That is why He placed His people in the land of Israel and wanted them to occupy the city of Gezer, which was an international crossroads.

Likewise, God wants you and me—His followers today—to live at the crossroads of life. He wants us to live so publicly that we become a "flavoring influence" on our culture. Rather than isolating ourselves from the world, God wants us to actively participate in and control areas that shape our culture and the world as a whole.

The crossroads at which I believe God wants me to make an impact is:

_____.

✏ 2.   *Israel failed to conquer the Gezers of their world and as a result failed in their mission to be God's witnesses to the world.*

We also fail in our mission as God's witnesses to the world when we don't take control and exert a godly influence on that which is significant in our culture.

What might be the consequences of your failure to be the witness God has called you to be? Be honest!

1. David clearly recognized that he stood at a crossroads and that he had a role to play in making the God of Israel known to the world. In what ways do you stand at a crossroads?

2. What could *you* do to publicly exert godly influence within your sphere of influence? In what arenas would God have you act to show that He is the Lord God?

3. How does God's call for you to exhibit Him in all that you do, think, and say affect what you do every day?

Action Points

Take a moment to review the key points you explored today. Then write down an action step (or steps) that you will commit to this week as a result of what you have learned.

1. *God wants His people to greatly influence the culture of their world.* That is why He placed His people in the land of Israel and wanted them to occupy the city of Gezer, which was an international crossroads.

   Likewise, God wants you and me—His followers today— to live at the crossroads of life. He wants us to live so publicly that we become a "flavoring influence" on our culture. Rather than isolating ourselves from the world, God wants us to actively participate in and control areas that shape our culture and the world as a whole.

   The crossroads at which I believe God wants me to make an impact is: _____

2. *Israel failed to conquer the Gezers of their world and as a result failed in their mission to be God's witnesses to the world.*

   We also fail in our mission as God's witnesses to the world when we don't take control and exert a godly influence on that which is significant in our culture.

   What might be the consequences of your failure to be the witness God has called you to be? Be honest!

3. *Just as the people of ancient Israel erected "standing stones" to commemorate God's supernatural actions on their behalf (such as when He gave them the Ten Commandments), God wants each of us to be a massebah—a living, standing stone.*

   In 1 Peter 2:4–5, we learn that we "like living stones are being built into a spiritual house." Each of us is like a piece of stone that God is shaping and cutting in order to build His kingdom. He wants us to exhibit Him to a watching world. As we live godly lives, non-Christians will see our good deeds and be drawn toward God—just as the people in ancient times were reminded about what God had done for them when they saw standing stones.

   What kind of standing stone are you? What about your life says to other people, "The Lord is God"?

   What specific action(s) could you take today to become a standing stone to other people in the future? Pray that God will empower you in that decision and watch as God becomes known to other people through you.

PLANNING NOTES:

✏ 3.   *Just as the people of ancient Israel erected "standing stones" to commemorate God's supernatural actions on their behalf (such as when He gave them the Ten Commandments), God wants each of us to be a massebah—a living, standing stone.*

In 1 Peter 2:4–5, we learn that we "like living stones are being built into a spiritual house." Each of us is like a piece of stone that God is shaping and cutting in order to build His kingdom. He wants us to exhibit Him to a watching world. As we live godly lives, non-Christians will see our good deeds and be drawn toward God—just as the people in ancient times were reminded about what God had done for them when they saw standing stones.

What kind of standing stone are you? What about your life says to other people, "The Lord is God"?

What specific action(s) could you take today to become a standing stone to other people in the future? Pray that God will empower you in that decision and watch as God becomes known to other people through you.

closing prayer

I minute

Dear God, thank You for putting us at the crossroads of life and giving us the opportunity to exert a godly influence and flavor our culture. Please give us the faith we need to be the witnesses You call us to be, to be living stones who testify that You, indeed, are God. Guide us this week as we try to put the truths we've just discovered into practice. Amen.

2. *Israel failed to conquer the Gezers of their world and as a result failed in their mission to be God's witnesses to the world.*

We also fail in our mission as God's witnesses to the world when we don't take control and exert a godly influence on that which is significant in our culture.

What might be the consequences of your failure to be the witness God has called you to be? Be honest!

3. *Just as the people of ancient Israel erected "standing stones" to commemorate God's supernatural actions on their behalf (such as when He gave them the Ten Commandments), God wants each of us to be a massebah—a living, standing stone.*

In 1 Peter 2:4–5, we learn that we "like living stones are being built into a spiritual house." Each of us is like a piece of stone that God is shaping and cutting in order to build His kingdom. He wants us to exhibit Him to a watching world. As we live godly lives, non-Christians will see our good deeds and be drawn toward God—just as the people in ancient times were reminded about what God had done for them when they saw standing stones.

What kind of standing stone are you? What about your life says to other people, "The Lord is God"?

What specific action(s) could you take today to become a standing stone to other people in the future? Pray that God will empower you in that decision and watch as God becomes known to other people through you.

PLANNING NOTES:

wet feet

Before You Lead

Synopsis

When you think of the Jordan River, what comes to mind? A wide river surging with power that races hundreds of miles toward the sea? If so, you're in for a surprise when you see this video. Mentioned 181 times in the Old Testament and 18 times in the New Testament, the Jordan River is certainly a prominent geographical feature of Israel. Yet it is only ninety miles from the Jordan's beginning point at the foot of Mount Hermon to its end at the Dead Sea. And in most places the river is a mere fifty to seventy-five feet across.

The Jordan River played an important, but in some ways unusual, role in the lives of the Israelites. Unlike many ancient peoples who considered the key rivers of their homelands to be sacred (such as the Ganges in India and the Nile in Egypt), the Israelites did not consider the Jordan River to be sacred. In fact, they considered it to be a barrier—an obstacle that had to be crossed in order to reach the land that God had promised them. This perspective is the source of the expression "to cross the Jordan," which means to pass through something that stands in the way.

Out of all the people in the world, God had selected the Jews to be His people. They were to live according to His ways in the land He would give them. They were to be His witnesses who would show the world what happens when a group of people live for Him with all their hearts. After they left Egypt and established the Torah covenant with God at Mount Sinai, the Jews approached the Promised Land but were afraid to venture in and possess the land. As punishment for their unbelief, they had to wander in the wilderness for forty years. When that time was over, they again approached the Promised Land. They gathered on the eastern side of the Jordan River near Jericho, ready to possess the land in which God had called them to be His witnesses. One barrier stood in their way, however—the Jordan River—and it was at flood stage! Imagine the Israelites encamped along the riverbank, wondering how they'd cross into their homeland.

No doubt this timing pleased the Canaanites. They worshiped fertility gods, particularly Baal whom they believed to be the god of water, rain, storm, wind, thunder, and lightning. In their minds, the flooded river demonstrated Baal's protection. God, however, was ready to declare that He commanded the forces of nature and was stronger than any false gods.

In Joshua 3, we read that the Israelites broke camp and prepared to move. The priests, carrying the ark of the covenant in which God's presence resided, went ahead of the people and stepped into the deep, swift Jordan River. Immediately, God stopped the water from flowing. The priests stood on dry ground in the middle of the river while all the Israelites passed them by.

During this session, you'll guide participants in understanding the significance of this crossing of the Jordan. Through that miracle, God overcame what stood between His people and their calling. But God did not act until the priests committed themselves totally to Him and stepped into the raging torrent. As soon as they made that complete, life-risking commitment and took those steps of faith, God used His power to divide the river.

Key Points of This Lesson

1. *The Israelites viewed the Jordan River as a barrier between them and the Promised Land where God had called them to live.* As Christians, we also face issues and obstacles that stand between us and the work to which God has called us.

2. *When the Israelites reached the banks of the Jordan River, they had to choose whether or not they would be totally committed to God.* They had to choose whether anything was outside of God's control and influence—including the barrier of raging water. They had to decide whether they would put their faith in the God who had led them through the desert or put their faith in the Canaanites' fertility gods who supposedly controlled water. Likewise, Christians today must be willing to be totally committed to God. We must not allow anything to stand between us and the calling God has placed before us. We must step out in faith in order for His power to be released in our lives.

3. *Jesus' baptism in the Jordan River symbolized God's creation of a new order—a new, loving, caring way of doing things that the Spirit of God was bringing to the world.* As followers of Jesus, we are God's ambassadors who are called to bring the healing, love, and comfort of God into the lives of broken people.

Session Outline (51 minutes)

I. Introduction (5 minutes)
Welcome
What's to Come
Questions to Think About

II. Show Video "Wet Feet" (17 minutes)

III. Group Discovery (20 minutes)
Video Highlights
Small Group Bible Discovery

IV. Faith Lesson (8 minutes)
Time for Reflection
Action Points

V. Closing Prayer (1 minute)

Materials

No additional materials are needed for this session. However, you may want to record participant's answers to the Questions to Think About on a marker board, chalkboard, or overhead projector. Otherwise, simply view the video prior to leading the session so you are familiar with its main points.

wet feet

introduction

5 minutes

Welcome

> Assemble the participants together. Welcome them to session two of *Faith Lessons on the Promised Land.*

What's to Come

In this session, we'll learn about the Jordan River—its size, its geographical importance, and what it symbolized to the Jews and to the Canaanites. We'll discover how the Jews finally crossed it and set foot in the Promised Land after wandering for forty years in the wilderness. Ray Vander Laan will challenge us to consider the barriers we face when we pursue God's calling for our lives. He will also encourage us to commit ourselves completely to God and to step out in faith and discover what God has in store for us.

Questions to Think About

> *Participant's Guide page 27.*

Before we begin the video, turn to page 27 of your Participant's Guide. Let's consider two key questions that relate to how we live out God's calling for our lives.

> Ask each question and solicit a few responses from group members. If desired, record participant's answers to these questions on a marker board, chalkboard, or overhead projector.

🖉 1. What are some of the barriers we allow to exist between us and the calling God has given us to fulfill? In other words, what keeps us from completely trusting Him and committing our lives to Him?

> *Suggested Responses:* fear that He will not really take care of us, fear that He will fail us, fear of rejection by other people, wanting to run our own lives, thinking that God doesn't want the best for us, uncertainty about our calling, fear that we won't be able to accomplish what God has called us to do, disobedience, etc.

🖉 2. How does who we believe God to be influence how much we trust Him in daily life?

SESSION TWO

wet feet

questions to think about

1. What are some of the barriers we allow to exist between us and the calling God has given us to fulfill? In other words, what keeps us from completely trusting Him and committing our lives to Him?

2. How does who we believe God to be influence how much we trust Him in daily life?

27

PLANNING NOTES:

Suggested Responses: If we believe He loves us, it'll be easier to trust Him. If we believe He is powerful enough to help us during the raging storms of life, it is easier to turn to Him for help. If, however, we don't believe He is who He claims to be, we won't want to trust Him. We will try to run our lives on our own and perhaps turn away from our calling.

Let's keep these ideas in mind as we view the video.

video presentation

Participant's Guide page 28.

17 minutes

On page 28 of your Participant's Guide, you will find a space in which to take notes on key points as we watch this video.

Leader's Video Observations

The Jordan River

Stepping into the Jordan

The Meaning of Jesus' Baptism

SESSION TWO

wet feet

questions to think about

1. What are some of the barriers we allow to exist between us and the calling God has given us to fulfill? In other words, what keeps us from completely trusting Him and committing our lives to Him?

2. How does who we believe God to be influence how much we trust Him in daily life?

27

28   Faith Lessons on the Promised Land

video notes

The Jordan River

Stepping into the Jordan

The Meaning of Jesus' Baptism

PLANNING NOTES:

group Discovery

20 minutes

> If your group has seven or more members, use the **Video Highlights** with the entire group (5 minutes), then break into small groups of three to five to discuss the **Small Group Bible Discovery** (10 minutes). Then reassemble the group to discuss the key points discovered (5 minutes).
>
> If your group has fewer than seven members, begin with the **Video Highlights** (5 minutes), then do one or more of the topics found in the **Small Group Bible Discovery** as a group (10 minutes). Finally, spend five minutes at the end discussing points that had an impact on participants.

Video Highlights (5 minutes)

> Here you'll ask one or more of the following questions that directly relate to the video the participants have just seen.

Look at the map of geographical features of the land of Israel on page 30 of your Participant's Guide.

> *Participant's Guide page 30.*

Note the Coastal Plain, the Shephelah, and the Central Mountains, with which we became familiar during the first session. In this session, our attention is drawn to the Great Rift Valley, particularly the Jordan River, which runs down the valley from the foot of Mount Hermon through the Sea of Galilee and into the Dead Sea. The children of Israel approached the Promised Land from the wilderness to the east, choosing to cross the Jordan River near Jericho, just north of the Dead Sea.

✏ 1. From the stories we've read in the Bible, most of us have an image of what the Jordan River looks like. What about the river surprised you when you saw it in the video?

Suggested Responses: Allow participants to share their perceptions with the group. Most people are surprised that the Jordan River isn't very wide and that it doesn't seem very challenging.

✏ 2. What did God demonstrate when He miraculously guided the Israelites across the Jordan River—and to whom?

Suggested Responses: God demonstrated His power, after the priests literally stepped into the water, to both the Israelites and the Canaanites. He showed that He alone controlled the power of nature, not Baal or other fertility gods worshiped by the Canaanites. He demonstrated that He was not only a desert God but was God of everything.

video Highlights

Look at the map of geographical features of the land of Israel on page 30. Note the coastal plain, the Shephelah, and the Central Mountains, with which we became familiar during the first session. In this session, our attention is drawn to the Great Rift Valley, particularly the Jordan River, which runs down the valley from the foot of Mount Hermon through the Sea of Galilee and into the Dead Sea. The children of Israel approached the Promised Land from the wilderness to the east, choosing to cross the Jordan River near Jericho, just north of the Dead Sea.

1. From the stories we've read in the Bible, most of us have an image of what the Jordan River looks like. What about the river surprised you when you saw it in the video?

2. What did God demonstrate when He miraculously guided the Israelites across the Jordan River—and to whom?

3. What similarities do you see between Jesus' baptism in the Jordan River and the Israelites' crossing of the Jordan in order to possess the Promised Land?

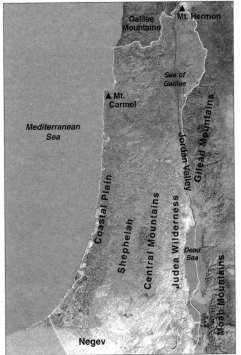

Topography of Israel

Galilee Mountains

▲ Mt. Hermon

Sea of Galilee

▲ Mt. Carmel

Mediterranean Sea

Jordan Valley

Gilead Mountains

Coastal Plain

Shephelah

Central Mountains

Judea Wilderness

Dead Sea

Moab Mountains

Negev

PLANNING NOTES:

✏ 3. What similarities do you see between Jesus' baptism in the Jordan River and the Israelites' crossing of the Jordan in order to possess the Promised Land?

Suggested Responses: Jesus came up out of the water to usher in a new order—a new way of living under the Spirit of God. The Israelites also came up out of the bed of the Jordan River to bring a new order—God's way of living—into the land God had given to them.

Topography of Israel

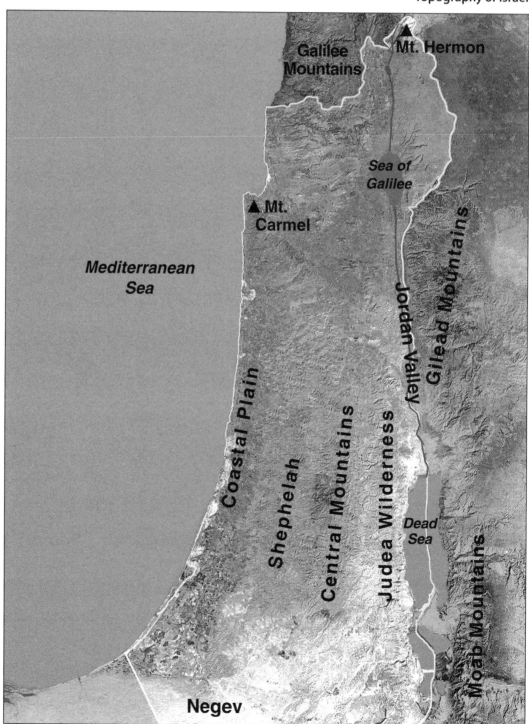

video highlights

Look at the map of geographical features of the land of Israel on page 30. Note the coastal plain, the Shephelah, and the Central Mountains, with which we became familiar during the first session. In this session, our attention is drawn to the Great Rift Valley, particularly the Jordan River, which runs down the valley from the foot of Mount Hermon through the Sea of Galilee and into the Dead Sea. The children of Israel approached the Promised Land from the wilderness to the east, choosing to cross the Jordan River near Jericho, just north of the Dead Sea.

1. From the stories we've read in the Bible, most of us have an image of what the Jordan River looks like. What about the river surprised you when you saw it in the video?

2. What did God demonstrate when He miraculously guided the Israelites across the Jordan River—and to whom?

3. What similarities do you see between Jesus' baptism in the Jordan River and the Israelites' crossing of the Jordan in order to possess the Promised Land?

30   Faith Lessons on the Promised Land

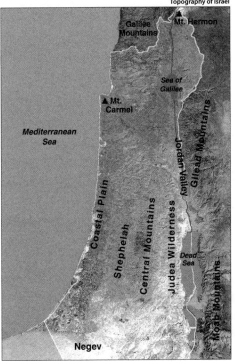

Topography of Israel

PLANNING NOTES:

Small Group Bible Discovery (10 minutes)

> *Participant's Guide pages 31–37.*
>
> During this time, a group with fewer than seven participants will stay together. A group of seven or more participants will break into small groups and reassemble as a large group during the final five minutes. Assign each group one of the following topics. If you have more than four small groups, assign some topics to more than one group.

Let's break into groups of three to five—people sitting near you—and study some of the Bible passages and truths mentioned in the video.

Turn to pages 31–37 in your Participant's Guide. There you'll find a list of four topics. You'll have ten minutes to read and discuss the topic I'll assign to you. Choose one person in your group to be a spokesperson for your group when we discuss these topics later.

> Assign each group a topic.

I'll signal you when one minute is left.

> After nine minutes, let participants know that they have one minute remaining. Then reassemble the entire group. After everyone is back together, begin asking one person from each small group to briefly share a key idea with the larger group. In some cases, you may not have time for every group to share their discoveries.

As time allows, let's briefly share the key ideas that your group discussed.

Topic A: Crossing the Jordan River

✏ 1. Each of the following Bible passages tells a story involving the Jordan River. Review each story and note the significant details that stand out to you.

    a. Deuteronomy 1:21–32; 3:23–28; 34:1–4

       Suggested Responses: When the Israelites refused to take possession of the land God had given to them, God refused to let them go in. He punished every Israelite twenty years or older for their unbelief—including Moses. Moses begged God to allow him to cross the Jordan River and go into the land, but God had a specific purpose for taking His people into the Promised Land and didn't allow Moses to go in alone. Moses had to be satisfied to look across the river.

    b. 1 Kings 16:29–33; 17:1–6

       Suggested Responses: After King Ahab of Israel engaged in great evil against God, Elijah the prophet told the king there would be a drought. Then God told Elijah to cross to the east side of the Jordan River and hide from the evil king. The river was a barrier of protection for Elijah.

small Group Bible Discovery

Topic A: Crossing the Jordan River

1. Each of the following Bible passages tells a story involving the Jordan River. Review each story and note the significant details that stand out to you.

   a. Deuteronomy 1:21–32; 3:23–28; 34:1–4

   b. 1 Kings 16:29–33; 17:1–6

   c. 2 Samuel 17:15–22

   d. 2 Kings 2:1–2, 5–15

PLANNING NOTES:

c. 2 Samuel 17:15–22

Suggested Responses: Absalom, David's rebellious son and the leader of Israel's army, schemed to kill King David and everyone who was loyal to him. But David, who was camped near the Jordan, was forewarned. David and his people arose during the night and crossed the Jordan River to safety. The river was a barrier of protection for David and his people.

d. 2 Kings 2:1–2, 5–15

Suggested Responses: Just before being taken up to heaven, Elijah walked toward the Jordan River, where the Lord had sent him. Elisha went with him, and when they came to the Jordan River, Elijah struck the water with his cloak. The water parted so they could walk across. After God took Elijah to heaven, Elisha used Elijah's cloak to again part the waters so he could return across the Jordan River. God again demonstrated His power over water and responded to Elisha's faith.

✏ 2. What common threads do you see in these stories?

Suggested Responses: It's important to be on the side of the Jordan that God wants you to be on; crossing the Jordan was essential to the fulfillment of God's work; God used the river to demonstrate His power and presence; God used the river to protect His people, etc.

DATA FILE

The Jordan River
- Starts in northern Israel at the foot of Mount Hermon, more than 1,500 feet above sea level, and ends almost 1,400 feet below sea level at the Dead Sea.
- Meanders for 200 miles from Mount Hermon to the Dead Sea, a distance of 90 miles as the crow flies.
- Flows through the Great Rift Valley, a cut in the earth's crust that extends all the way to Lake Victoria in southern Africa.
- Received its name from a Hebrew word that means "to descend, to go down" because the river descends from the slopes of Mount Hermon (which stands 9,000 feet above sea level) to the Dead Sea (nearly 1,400 feet below sea level).
- Is one of the fastest-flowing rivers for its size in the world.
- Is today dammed up where it runs out of the Sea of Galilee to help meet the State of Israel's water needs.

small Group Bible Discovery

Topic A: Crossing the Jordan River

1. Each of the following Bible passages tells a story involving the Jordan River. Review each story and note the significant details that stand out to you.

   a. Deuteronomy 1:21–32; 3:23–28; 34:1–4

   b. 1 Kings 16:29–33; 17:1–6

   c. 2 Samuel 17:15–22

   d. 2 Kings 2:1–2, 5–15

2. What common threads do you see in these stories?

DATA FILE

The Jordan River
- Starts in northern Israel at the foot of Mount Hermon, more than 1,500 feet above sea level, and ends almost 1,400 feet below sea level at the Dead Sea.
- Meanders for 200 miles from Mount Hermon to the Dead Sea, a distance of 90 miles as the crow flies.
- Flows through the Great Rift Valley, a cut in the earth's crust that extends all the way to Lake Victoria in southern Africa.
- Is one of the fastest-flowing rivers for its size in the world.
- Is today dammed up where it runs out of the Sea of Galilee to help meet the State of Israel's water needs.

Topic B: Commitment Means Making the First Move

Many Christians today are reluctant to step out in faith to pursue the calling God has given to them. As you read the following Scripture passages, take note of what making a commitment to follow God's calling required.

1. Read Joshua 3:5–17. Who was required to take action when the Israelites crossed the Jordan River? What was the result?

PLANNING NOTES:

Topic B: Commitment Means Making the First Move

Many Christians today are reluctant to step out in faith to pursue the calling God has given to them. As you read the following Scripture passages, take note of what making a commitment to follow God's calling required.

1. Read Joshua 3:5–17. Who was required to take action when the Israelites crossed the Jordan River? What was the result?

    Suggested Responses: Joshua—instructed the priests. Priests—carried the ark of the covenant into the Jordan and stood there. The people—followed the priests and crossed the Jordan on dry land. When the people stepped out in faith, God responded.

2. In faith, what did Joshua tell the people? (See Joshua 3:5.)

    Suggested Response: to prepare themselves spiritually because the next day God was going to do amazing things.

3. What did God reveal to Joshua? (See Joshua 3:7–8.)

    Suggested Responses: He would exalt Joshua by demonstrating His presence with him. Then He gave Joshua instructions for crossing the river that he was to convey to the priests.

4. What were some of God's reasons for enabling the Israelites to cross the Jordan River? (See Joshua 3:10.)

    Suggested Responses: God wanted them to know that He—the living God—was among them, that He would drive out the pagan tribes that lived in the Promised Land. He knew they needed more faith in who He was and what He would do for them.

The Ark of the Covenant

2. What common threads do you see in these stories?

DATA FILE

The Jordan River

- Starts in northern Israel at the foot of Mount Hermon, more than 1,500 feet above sea level, and ends almost 1,400 feet below sea level at the Dead Sea.
- Meanders for 200 miles from Mount Hermon to the Dead Sea, a distance of 90 miles as the crow flies.
- Flows through the Great Rift Valley, a cut in the earth's crust that extends all the way to Lake Victoria in southern Africa.
- Is one of the fastest-flowing rivers for its size in the world.
- Is today dammed up where it runs out of the Sea of Galilee to help meet the State of Israel's water needs.

Topic B: Commitment Means Making the First Move

Many Christians today are reluctant to step out in faith to pursue the calling God has given to them. As you read the following Scripture passages, take note of what making a commitment to follow God's calling required.

1. Read Joshua 3:5–17. Who was required to take action when the Israelites crossed the Jordan River? What was the result?

---

2. In faith, what did Joshua tell the people? (See Joshua 3:5.)

3. What did God reveal to Joshua? (See Joshua 3:7–8.)

4. What were some of God's reasons for enabling the Israelites to cross the Jordan River? (See Joshua 3:10.)

The Ark of the Covenant

✏ 5.   Clearly God could have divided the Jordan River at any time He chose. Why do you think He waited until the priests entered the water carrying the ark?

Suggested Responses: He wanted to teach His people the importance of stepping out in faith, in trusting Him even when circumstances seem to indicate that such steps won't make any difference. He wanted to emphasize the importance of personal commitment and its relationship to His demonstration of power and blessing.

✏ 6.   Write out your own "wet feet" concept—what it really means for you to follow God and pursue His calling.

Suggested Response: Encourage participants to describe in their own words the "plunge" they need to take in order for God to fulfill His plan through them.

Topic C: The Ark of God

The ark of the covenant became the focal point of God's presence among His people. It was so important to God that He described its construction before describing any other sacred object—even before the tabernacle (Exodus 25:10–22).

✏ 1.   What was the ark of the covenant's central purpose? (See Exodus 25:16.) What other purpose did it serve? (See Exodus 25:22.)

Suggested Responses: to hold the testimony (the Ten Commandments) that God would give to Moses. In addition, it often was the place where God would meet with Moses to give His commandments to His people.

✏ 2.   On the Day of Atonement (Yom Kippur), the great holy day of the Bible, what would happen? (See Leviticus 16:2.)

Suggested Responses: According to the pattern established by Aaron, the high priest would enter the Holy of Holies chamber in front of the ark, and God would appear in a cloud over the cover. A person who came before the ark was entering into God's presence, and only the high priest was allowed to come before the ark, and then only on the Day of Atonement. Any other appearance before the ark would result in the trespasser's death.

✏ 3.   What did the ark of the covenant symbolize to the people? (See Psalm 91:4; 99:1.)

Suggested Responses: His throne. It represented God's ruling power over all things; it was also a shield of protection that provided refuge for His people.

✏ 4.   During the siege of Jericho, where was the ark of the covenant carried? What did this symbolize? (See Joshua 6:1–11.)

Suggested Responses: Following in the footsteps of armed guards, the priests who carried the ark of the covenant around Jericho's walls were then followed by the Israelite army. This demonstrated that God Himself was in the midst of His chosen people as they went out to conquer the city.

5. Clearly God could have divided the Jordan River at any time He chose. Why do you think He waited until the priests entered the water carrying the ark?

6. Write out your own "wet feet" concept—what it really means for you to follow God and pursue His calling.

Topic C: The Ark of God

The ark of the covenant became the focal point of God's presence among His people. It was so important to God that He described its construction before describing any other sacred object—even before the tabernacle (Exodus 25:10–22).

1. What was the ark of the covenant's central purpose? (See Exodus 25:16.) What other purpose did it serve? (See Exodus 25:22.)

2. On the Day of Atonement (Yom Kippur), the great holy day of the Bible, what would happen? (See Leviticus 16:2.)

3. What did the ark of the covenant symbolize to the people? (See Psalm 91:4; 99:1.)

4. During the siege of Jericho, where was the ark of the covenant carried? What did this symbolize? (See Joshua 6:1–11.)

DATA FILE

The Ark of the Covenant:

- Was made of acacia wood, an extremely hard wood common to the Sinai Peninsula.
- Was three feet nine inches long, two feet three inches wide, and two feet three inches tall.
- Was gold plated and had a gold rim around the top.
- Stood on four legs, and on each side were two gold rings in which poles were inserted so the Levites (the priestly tribe) could carry it.
- Had a cover—called the mercy seat or atonement seat—that was made of pure gold. On top of the lid were two cherubim—probably sphinxes—whose wings stretched over the cover.
- Was viewed by the Israelites as God's footstool (1 Chronicles 28:2).

PLANNING NOTES:

DATA FILE

The Ark of the Covenant
- Was made of acacia wood, an extremely hard wood common to the Sinai Peninsula.
- Was three feet nine inches long, two feet three inches wide, and two feet three inches tall.
- Was gold plated and had a gold rim around the top.
- Stood on four legs, and on each side were two gold rings in which poles were inserted so the Levites (the priestly tribe) could carry it.
- Had a cover—called the mercy seat or atonement seat—that was made of pure gold. On top of the lid were two cherubim—probably sphinxes—whose wings stretched over the cover.
- Was viewed by the Israelites as God's footstool (1 Chronicles 28:2).

✏ 5. Years later, even the priests of Israel became unfaithful and dishonored God (1 Samuel 2:27–36), so God ceased to honor His people and removed His strength from them. Read 1 Samuel 4:1–11 and list the consequences that followed. What did the Israelites depend on to save them? Why do you think their efforts failed?

Suggested Responses: God allowed the Philistine army to defeat the Israelite army. In response, the Israelites brought the ark of the covenant into their camp to the place of battle. They were encouraged, but God did not use His power on their behalf. They suffered a great defeat and the loss of about 30,000 soldiers. The Philistines captured the ark, and both of Eli's sons died. God's power had brought great blessing and had dramatically defeated Israel's enemies in the past, when they faithfully followed Him, but God did not honor His people when they refused to honor Him.

✏ 6. According to 1 Corinthians 3:16–17, where does God choose to reveal Himself today?

Suggested Response: God's Spirit resides in the people who have accepted Jesus the Messiah as their Savior and Lord. They are now His holy temple, and God reveals Himself through them.

DID YOU KNOW?
Following Middle Eastern custom, God instructed Moses to make two summary documents of the covenant He made with His people. These documents (each of which contained all Ten Commandments) were His guarantee that His Word would never fail. Normally, each covenanting party took a summary copy of the covenant and placed it in their most sacred place, where it would be read regularly as a reminder of the covenant.

Apparently God gave both copies to Moses, ordering him to place them into the ark. Imagine Moses' reaction when he learned that the most sacred place for God and for Israel was the same—the ark of the covenant!

3. What did the ark of the covenant symbolize to the people? (See Psalm 91:4; 99:1.)

4. During the siege of Jericho, where was the ark of the covenant carried? What did this symbolize? (See Joshua 6:1–11.)

DATA FILE

The Ark of the Covenant:
- Was made of acacia wood, an extremely hard wood common to the Sinai Peninsula.
- Was three feet nine inches long, two feet three inches wide, and two feet three inches tall.
- Was gold plated and had a gold rim around the top.
- Stood on four legs, and on each side were two gold rings in which poles were inserted so the Levites (the priestly tribe) could carry it.
- Had a cover—called the mercy seat or atonement seat—that was made of pure gold. On top of the lid were two cherubim—probably sphinxes—whose wings stretched over the cover.
- Was viewed by the Israelites as God's footstool (1 Chronicles 28:2).

5. Years later, even the priests of Israel became unfaithful and dishonored God (1 Samuel 2:27–36), so God ceased to honor His people and removed His strength from them. Read 1 Samuel 4:1–11, and list the consequences that followed. What did the Israelites depend on to save them? Why do you think their efforts failed?

6. According to 1 Corinthians 3:16–17, where does God choose to reveal Himself today?

DID YOU KNOW?

Following Middle Eastern custom, God instructed Moses to make two summary documents of the covenant He made with His people. These documents (each of which contained all Ten Commandments) were His guarantee that His Word would never fail. Normally, each covenanting party took a summary copy of the covenant and placed it in their most sacred place, where it would be read regularly as a reminder of the covenant.

Apparently God gave both copies to Moses, ordering him to place them into the ark. Imagine Moses' reaction when he learned that the most sacred place for God and for Israel was the same—the ark of the covenant!

PLANNING NOTES:

Topic D: Up, Out of the Jordan: The Baptism of Jesus

The greatest New Testament event to take place in relationship to the Jordan River was the baptism of Jesus.

1. Consider the parallels between the symbolism of Jesus' baptism and the creation story:

The Water	Genesis 1:2	was formless and represented chaos
	Matthew 3:16	Jesus descended into the water, which represented chaos and death
The Spirit	Genesis 1:2	hovered and moved over the water
	Matthew 3:16	The Spirit of God descended upon Jesus and moved with Him
God's Approval	Genesis 1:31	God was pleased with the goodness of His creation
	Matthew 3:17	God was pleased with Jesus, His beloved Son
A New Creation	Genesis 1:3–30	Out of the formless void, God made a new world that had never existed before
	Matthew 11:2–6	Jesus came up out of the waters of the Jordan to usher in a new creation, a new world order in which love and healing would prevail over evil
Temptation	Genesis 3:1–7	Satan soon tempted Adam and Eve
	Matthew 4:1–11	Jesus was led immediately into the wilderness to face Satan's temptation

2. Why do you think Jesus said that His followers would be "greater" than John the Baptist? (See Luke 7:28.)

Suggested Responses: John the Baptist preceded the new creation that Jesus instituted. Jesus' followers were called to be the agents of this new creation, to teach and to demonstrate a new way of living in the power of Jesus' love.

3. In John 14:9–13, Jesus answers a question and in so doing explains His calling. What was His calling? How does it compare to the calling of the Israelites as they went in to possess the Promised Land?

Suggested Responses: Jesus came to reveal the Father; thus to see and know Jesus is to know God. By living according to God's initiative, Jesus would accomplish God's works in the world. His purpose was to glorify God. That was also the calling and mission of the children of Israel in the Promised Land. It is also the calling and mission of every Christian.

Topic D: Up, Out of the Jordan: The Baptism of Jesus

The greatest New Testament event to take place in relationship to the Jordan River was the baptism of Jesus.

1. Consider the parallels between the symbolism of Jesus' baptism and the creation story:

The Water	Genesis 1:2	
	Matthew 3:16	
The Spirit	Genesis 1:2	
	Matthew 3:16	
God's Approval	Genesis 1:31	
	Matthew 3:17	
A New Creation	Genesis 1:3–30	
	Matthew 11:2–6	
Temptation	Genesis 3:1–7	
	Matthew 4:1–11	

2. Why do you think Jesus said that His followers would be "greater" than John the Baptist? (See Luke 7:28.)

3. In John 14:9–13, Jesus answers a question and in so doing explains His calling. What was His calling? How does it compare to the calling of the Israelites as they went in to possess the Promised Land?

faith Lesson

Time for Reflection (4 minutes)

It's time for each of us to think quietly about how we can apply what we've learned today. On page 38 of the Participant's Guide, you'll find a passage of Scripture. Let's each read this passage silently and take the next few minutes to reflect on the questions that follow the Scripture passage.

Please do not talk during this time. It's a time when we can consider the obstacles that stand between us and God's calling on our lives. It's a time to take seriously our commitment to God's plan for our lives.

> *The Scripture passage and questions are reproduced in their entirety in the Participant's Guide on pages 38–42.*

Joshua said to the Israelites, "Come here and listen to the words of the LORD your God. This is how you will know that the living God is among you and that he will certainly drive out before you the Canaanites, Hittites, Hivites, Perizzites, Girgashites, Amorites and Jebusites. See, the ark of the covenant of the Lord of all the earth will go into the Jordan ahead of you. Now then, choose twelve men from the tribes of Israel, one from each tribe. And as soon as the priests who carry the ark of the LORD—the Lord of all the earth—set foot in the Jordan, its waters flowing downstream will be cut off and stand up in a heap."

So when the people broke camp to cross the Jordan, the priests carrying the ark of the covenant went ahead of them. Now the Jordan is at flood stage all during harvest. Yet as soon as the priests who carried the ark reached the Jordan and their feet touched the water's edge, the water from upstream stopped flowing. It piled up in a heap a great distance away, at a town called Adam in the vicinity of Zarethan, while the water flowing down to the Sea of the Arabah (the Salt Sea) was completely cut off. So the people crossed over opposite Jericho. The priests who carried the ark of the covenant of the LORD stood firm on dry ground in the middle of the Jordan, while all Israel passed by until the whole nation had completed the crossing on dry ground.

JOSHUA 3:9–17

1. Take a moment to imagine what it was like for the Israelites to stand on the banks of the Jordan River on that glorious day. Imagine their excitement—a new homeland. Imagine their fear—they didn't know what awaited them. Imagine their anticipation—what would God do? His ark was headed into floodwaters! Imagine their awe—to walk across the Jordan River on dry land.

2. Imagine that you are standing on the banks of the Jordan River and the land on the other side represents your life's mission or a specific task God has given you. What represents the "Jordan River," the barrier in your life that keeps you from entering into the life God intends for you? How might you take a step of faith to cross over that "Jordan River" in your life?

Faith Lesson

Time for Reflection

Read the following passage of Scripture silently and take the next few minutes to consider the obstacles that stand between you and God's calling on your life.

> Joshua said to the Israelites, "Come here and listen to the words of the LORD your God. This is how you will know that the living God is among you and that he will certainly drive out before you the Canaanites, Hittites, Hivites, Perizzites, Girgashites, Amorites and Jebusites. See, the ark of the covenant of the Lord of all the earth will go into the Jordan ahead of you. Now then, choose twelve men from the tribes of Israel, one from each tribe. And as soon as the priests who carry the ark of the LORD—the Lord of all the earth—set foot in the Jordan, its waters flowing downstream will be cut off and stand up in a heap."
>
> So when the people broke camp to cross the Jordan, the priests carrying the ark of the covenant went ahead of them. Now the Jordan is at flood stage all during harvest. Yet as soon as the priests who carried the ark reached the Jordan and their feet touched the water's edge, the water from upstream stopped flowing. It piled up in a heap a great distance away, at a town called Adam in the vicinity of Zarethan, while the water flowing down to the Sea of the Arabah (the Salt Sea) was completely cut off. So the people crossed over opposite Jericho. The priests who carried the ark of the covenant of the LORD stood firm on dry ground in the middle of the Jordan, while all Israel passed by until the whole nation had completed the crossing on dry ground.
>
> JOSHUA 3:9–17

1. Take a moment to imagine what it was like for the Israelites to stand on the banks of the Jordan River on that glorious day. Imagine their excitement—a new homeland. Imagine their fear—they didn't know what awaited them. Imagine their

anticipation—what would God do? His ark was headed into floodwaters! Imagine their awe—to walk across the Jordan River on dry land.

2. Imagine that you are standing on the banks of the Jordan River and the land on the other side represents your life's mission or a specific task God has given you. What represents the "Jordan River," the barrier in your life that keeps you from entering into the life God intends for you? How might you take a step of faith to cross over that "Jordan River" in your life?

3. Think of a time in your life, or in the life of someone you know, where a total commitment to God brought about a great display of His power and blessing. How can that testimony of God's love and faithfulness be a "standing stone" for you that will encourage you to pursue God's calling for your life?

Action Points

Take a moment to review the key points you explored today. Then, determine the step (or steps) of commitment that you will take this week to carry out God's calling in your life.

1. *The Israelites viewed the Jordan River as a barrier between them and the Promised Land where God had called them to live.* As Christians, we also face issues and obstacles that stand between us and the work to which God has called us.

   Think about your life. What is the barrier that keeps you from making a total commitment to God?

✏ 3.   Think of a time in your life, or in the life of someone you know, where a total commitment to God brought about a great display of His power and blessing. How can that testimony of God's love and faithfulness be a "standing stone" for you that will encourage you to pursue God's calling for your life?

> As soon as participants have spent four minutes reflecting on the above questions, get the entire group's attention and move to the next section.

Action Points (4 minutes)

> *The following points are reproduced on pages 39–42 of the Participant's Guide:*

Now it's time to wrap up our session.

> Give participants a moment to transition from their thoughtfulness to giving you their full attention.

I'd like to take a moment to summarize the key points we explored. After I have reviewed each point, I will give you a moment to determine the step (or steps) of commitment that you will take this week to carry out God's calling in your life.

> Read each point and pause after each so that participants can consider and write out their commitment.

✏ 1.   *The Israelites viewed the Jordan River as a barrier between them and the Promised Land where God had called them to live.* As Christians, we also face issues and obstacles that stand between us and the work to which God has called us.

Think about your life. What is the barrier that keeps you from making a total commitment to God?

What about that barrier is so frightening to you that you fail to put your complete trust in God? Do you truly believe that barrier is beyond God's influence?

✏ 2.   *When the Israelites reached the banks of the Jordan River, they had to choose whether or not they would be totally committed to God.* They had to choose whether anything was outside of God's control and influence—including the barrier of raging water. They had to decide whether they would put their faith in the God who had led them through the desert or put their faith in the Canaanites' fertility gods who supposedly controlled water.

Likewise, Christians today must be willing to be totally committed to God. We must not allow anything to stand between us and the calling God has placed before us. We must step out in faith in order for His power to be released in our lives.

anticipation—what would God do? His ark was headed into floodwaters! Imagine their awe—to walk across the Jordan River on dry land.

2. Imagine that you are standing on the banks of the Jordan River and the land on the other side represents your life's mission or a specific task God has given you. What represents the "Jordan River," the barrier in your life that keeps you from entering into the life God intends for you? How might you take a step of faith to cross over that "Jordan River" in your life?

3. Think of a time in your life, or in the life of someone you know, where a total commitment to God brought about a great display of His power and blessing. How can that testimony of God's love and faithfulness be a "standing stone" for you that will encourage you to pursue God's calling for your life?

Action Points

Take a moment to review the key points you explored today. Then, determine the step (or steps) of commitment that you will take this week to carry out God's calling in your life.

1. *The Israelites viewed the Jordan River as a barrier between them and the Promised Land where God had called them to live.* As Christians, we also face issues and obstacles that stand between us and the work to which God has called us.

   Think about your life. What is the barrier that keeps you from making a total commitment to God?

What about that barrier is so frightening to you that you fail to put your complete trust in God? Do you truly believe that barrier is beyond God's influence?

2. *When the Israelites reached the banks of the Jordan River, they had to choose whether or not they would be totally committed to God.* They had to choose whether anything was outside of God's control and influence—including the barrier of raging water. They had to decide whether they would put their faith in the God who had led them through the desert or put their faith in the Canaanites' fertility gods who supposedly controlled water.

   Likewise, Christians today must be willing to be totally committed to God. We must not allow anything to stand between us and the calling God has placed before us. We must step out in faith in order for His power to be released in our lives.

   The priests took a step of faith into the flooded Jordan River and saw God do a miracle. What step of faith can you, your family, and/or your church take so that God's power can be more visible in your community? How, in other words, might you "get your feet wet"?

PLANNING NOTES:

The priests took a step of faith into the flooded Jordan River and saw God do a miracle. What step of faith can you, your family, and/or your church take so that God's power can be more visible in your community? How, in other words, might you "get your feet wet"?

✏ 3.   *Jesus' baptism in the Jordan River symbolized God's creation of a new order—a new, loving, caring way of doing things that the Spirit of God was bringing to the world.* As followers of Jesus, we are God's ambassadors who are called to bring the healing, love, and comfort of God into the lives of broken people.

What are the issues, concerns, problems, or aspects of your community in which God would have you serve as His ambassador? In what way might you bring Christ's restoring, healing love to a hurting individual in your community? What step of faith could you take this week to actively rely on His power?

FAITH PROFILE

Deceived by Appearances

The Great Rift Valley, through which the Jordan River flows, is arid and has poor soil that absorbs little water and will not sustain vegetation. Along the river, however, the soil is suitable for vegetation, and dense plants grow. This lush growth, which the Bible refers to as the "thickets of the Jordan" (Jeremiah 49:19; Zechariah 11:3), does not extend far from the water's edge.

A spring probably created the lush oasis that Lot saw as he surveyed the land from the edge of the Judea Wilderness near Bethel (Genesis 13:10–13). He "looked up and saw that the whole plain of the Jordan was well watered." As we know from Scripture, however, the most obvious choice isn't always the best one—or the one that pleases the Lord.

When Lot left Abraham, he not only left the wilderness, where a person had to depend on God for survival, but chose to leave Abraham's God. That, in turn, spelled disaster for Lot and his family. In his greed, Lot had chosen what appeared to be the best land, but the watered portion of the riverbed was too small and dense for his flocks, and the plains along the river lacked the vegetation necessary to sustain life. So Lot's solution was to move to the well-watered, pagan city of Sodom where he became a leader among idolatrous people who worshiped the Canaanite fertility gods and practiced all forms of sexual perversion. He "sat in the gate" of Sodom in a position of honor, and only God's mercy and the loyalty of his uncle Abraham allowed him and his daughters to escape God's judgment.

After losing everything else dear to him, including his wife, Lot discovered that even his daughters had become like the people of Sodom (Genesis 19:30–38). His grandchildren became the people of Moab and Ammon, infamous in the Bible for their idolatry and evil ways.

Lot's profile serves as a reminder to us. Our culture may appear to be desirable and healthful, making it easy for us to become caught up in secular society's values and practices. The only way to be free of today's "Sodoms," however, is to make choices according to God's standards. Abraham knew this lesson well.

3. *Jesus' baptism in the Jordan River symbolized God's creation of a new order—a new, loving, caring way of doing things that the Spirit of God was bringing to the world.* As followers of Jesus, we are God's ambassadors who are called to bring the healing, love, and comfort of God into the lives of broken people.

What are the issues, concerns, problems, or aspects of your community in which God would have you serve as His ambassador? In what way might you bring Christ's restoring, healing love to a hurting individual in your community? What step of faith could you take this week to actively rely on His power?

42 Faith Lessons on the Promised Land

FAITH PROFILE

Deceived by Appearances

The Great Rift Valley, through which the Jordan River flows, is arid and has poor soil that absorbs little water and will not sustain vegetation. Along the river, however, the soil is suitable for vegetation, and dense plants grow. This lush growth, which the Bible refers to as the "thickets of the Jordan" (Jeremiah 49:19; Zechariah 11:3), does not extend far from the water's edge.

A spring probably created the lush oasis that Lot saw as he surveyed the land from the edge of the Judea Wilderness near Bethel (Genesis 13:10–13). He "looked up and saw that the whole plain of the Jordan was well watered." As we know from Scripture, however, the most obvious choice isn't always the best one—or the one that pleases the Lord.

When Lot left Abraham, he not only left the wilderness, where a person had to depend on God for survival, but chose to leave Abraham's God. That, in turn, spelled disaster for Lot and his family. In his greed, Lot had chosen what appeared to be the best land, but the watered portion of the riverbed was too small and dense for his flocks, and the plains along the river lacked the vegetation necessary to sustain life. So Lot's solution was to move to the well-watered, pagan city of Sodom where he became a leader among idolatrous people who worshiped the Canaanite fertility gods and practiced all forms of sexual perversion. He "sat in the gate" of Sodom in a position of honor, and only God's mercy and the loyalty of his uncle Abraham allowed him and his daughters to escape God's judgment.

After losing everything else dear to him, including his wife, Lot discovered that even his daughters had become like the people of Sodom (Genesis 19:30–38). His grandchildren became the people of Moab and Ammon, infamous in the Bible for their idolatry and evil ways.

Lot's profile serves as a reminder to us. Our culture may appear to be desirable and healthful, making it easy for us to become caught up in secular society's values and practices. The only way to be free of today's "Sodoms," however, is to make choices according to God's standards. Abraham knew this lesson well.

PLANNING NOTES:

closing prayer

I minute

I hope that this faith lesson has been as meaningful and challenging to you as it has been to me. Let's leave here today with a renewed commitment to live out the calling God has placed on our hearts.

Dear God, thank You for showing us today the power of faith and how important it is for us to get our feet wet in total commitment to You. Please help us to be positive influences in our culture as a result of knowing You and receiving the courage to step out in faith. Help us to become Your agents who, like Jesus, are willing to reach out to the poor, the hurting, the sick, and the spiritually blind. Amen.

PLANNING NOTES:

first fruits

Before You Lead

Synopsis

In this video, you'll discover some of the fascinating history of Jericho. The lowest city in the world (located more than 1,000 feet below sea level), Jericho also appears to be the world's oldest city—dating back to more than 8,000 B.C. How old is that? Well, by the time Abraham passed by the city, it was already about 7,000 years old!

The tel of Jericho stands at the opening of a mountain pass near the northern end of the Dead Sea. The city was watered by Elisha's Spring, which still flows out to form a beautiful, lush oasis in the Jordan Valley. Once a thriving metropolis, it was situated on the strategic road linking the Via Maris and the King's Highway—the major trade routes of the ancient world. This fortified city played a prominent role in various Bible stories and events. Ray Vander Laan explores two of them in this video—the stories of Rahab and how God delivered the city of Jericho into the Israelites' hands.

After wandering in the wilderness for forty years, the Israelites were finally ready to possess the land God had promised to give them. So, following the trade routes, they came up from the Negev Desert along the King's Highway and crossed the Jordan River at Jericho. Their first obstacle in possessing the land was the city of Jericho.

In order to learn about Jericho, the Israelites sent spies into the city. Rahab, a prostitute, hid them on her roof so they wouldn't be captured. After telling the spies how afraid her people became when they heard the Israelites were coming, Rahab confessed that "the Lord your God is God in heaven and on earth." That's quite a statement for a prostitute living in a pagan city! Clearly the people of Israel were demonstrating by their conduct that God is God. Because of her faith, Rahab and her family were saved when the Israelites captured Jericho. Even more important, Rahab is one of four women God mentions in the ancestral lineage of Jesus the Messiah!

When it came time to conquer the city of Jericho, the angel of the Lord appeared to Joshua—the Israelites' leader—and revealed God's battle strategy. As Joshua discovered, the upcoming battle with Jericho was God's battle. God was orchestrating His will, and the Israelites were simply His instruments in that process. The Israelites followed God's unusual battle plan, and God brought about a miraculous victory. As a result, the pagan inhabitants of the Promised Land feared the Israelites' God.

But the Canaanites weren't the only ones who learned more about God through this victory. God communicated a message to the Israelites as well. As God's people, they were to acknowledge that He was the giver of all they had.

They customarily acknowledged this truth by giving to God the first portion of their crops, the "first fruits," as a symbol of their trust in Him to provide for their future needs. God required them to apply the principle of "first fruits" to the conquest of Jericho.

When the Israelites entered the Promised Land, they owned nothing. They had conquered Jericho with God's help, so He wanted them to demonstrate that they knew He had enabled them to conquer the city, to remember that everything they had came from Him, and to trust Him to provide the rest of the land. God wanted Jericho's ruins to be the Israelites' "first fruits" offering to Him. He wanted the ruins to be left as a testimony that the land belonged to Him and that those who lived in it sought to serve Him. Thus God stated that the sons of anyone who rebuilt Jericho would die.

This prophecy came true years later when Hiel rebuilt Jericho (1 Kings 16:33–34). By rebuilding Jericho, Hiel took what belonged to the Lord in order to use it for himself. He paid for that sin against God with the lives of his sons.

The story of Jericho offers an important lesson for us today. God has called His people to be special, holy people. He has not provided for us purely for our benefit. We have been given what we have been given for His service and glory. May we never forget that what has been set apart for God belongs to Him.

Key Points of This Lesson

1. *As the Israelites took possession of the Promised Land, God clearly demonstrated that the battle against its pagan inhabitants was His battle, not theirs.*

   Likewise, as we seek to bring God's value system into our culture and to confront that which is contrary to God's way, we need to remember that the battle is the Lord's. He is the one who seeks to reclaim the world He created, and we are His instruments in that process.

2. *God's people are to follow the Old Testament principle of "first fruits," meaning we are to offer God the first part of what we receive as our provision.* By doing so, we acknowledge that God is the source of our provision and that we trust Him to continue to provide for us.

   If we give ourselves to God as His holy, "set-apart" people, He will take care of the rest! But if we use what has been set apart for God's use to benefit ourselves, we break the first-fruits principle. God does not provide for us so that we can honor ourselves. God gives us what we have—money, time, talents, etc.—so that He can use us as agents in His service.

Session Outline (52 minutes)

    I. Introduction (5 minutes)
    Welcome
    What's to Come
    Questions to Think About

    II. Show Video "Tel Jericho: First Fruits" (16 minutes)

    III. Group Discovery (20 minutes)
    Video Highlights
    Small Group Bible Discovery

    IV. Faith Lesson (10 minutes)
    Time for Reflection
    Action Points

    V. Closing Prayer (1 minute)

Materials

No additional materials are needed for this session. Simply view the video prior to leading the session so you are familiar with its main points.

PLANNING NOTES:

First Fruits

Introduction

5 minutes

Welcome

> Assemble the participants together. Welcome them to session three of *Faith Lessons on the Promised Land*.

What's to Come

After the Israelites crossed the Jordan River, they had to conquer the city of Jericho. During that first battle to take possession of the Promised Land, they learned crucial lessons about fighting God's battles and what it meant to acknowledge that God was the giver of all they had and to trust Him to meet their needs. As we Christians confront ungodly aspects of our culture, we'll face struggles and spiritual battles as well. Like the children of Israel, we must choose whether or not we will recognize God's provision in our lives and trust Him to provide for our future needs.

Questions to Think About

> *Participant's Guide page 43.*

Turn to page 43 of the Participant's Guide. Let's consider several questions that relate to the obstacles and battles God's people face when bringing God's way of living to bear on the world's culture.

> Ask each question and solicit a few responses from group members.

1. How might you have felt if you were one of the Israelites who had crossed the Jordan River into the Promised Land and had immediately encountered the fortified city of Jericho?

   Suggested Responses: fearful, wondered what God would do, questioned why God had brought us in this way, overwhelmed, intimidated, might have thought the oasis was good enough, might have wanted to "make peace" and coexist, etc.

SESSION THREE

first fruits

questions to think about

1. How might you have felt if you were one of the Israelites who had crossed the Jordan River into the Promised Land and had immediately encountered the fortified city of Jericho?

2. What are some of the intimidating, well-established, evil aspects of our society that Christians must confront if they follow God's calling and seek to bring His standards to bear on society?

3. Consider what is required to stand up and battle against the established evils of our society. In what ways are your feelings similar to or unlike what you imagine you would have felt as an Israelite facing Jericho?

43

PLANNING NOTES:

✍ 2. What are some of the intimidating, well-established, evil aspects of our society that Christians must confront if they follow God's calling and seek to bring His standards to bear on society?

Suggested Responses: pornography, crime, sexual infidelity, abortion, injustice, racial hatred, immoral lifestyles, abuse, greed, self-righteousness, etc.

✍ 3. Consider what is required to stand up and battle against the established evils of our society. In what ways are your feelings similar to or unlike what you imagine you would have felt as an Israelite facing Jericho?

Suggested Responses: Allow participants to share their perspectives.

Let's keep these ideas in mind as we watch the video.

video presentation

16 minutes

| Participant's Guide page 44. |

On page 44 of your Participant's Guide, you will find a space in which to take notes on key points as we watch this video.

Leader's Video Observations

The City of Jericho

Rahab

God's Battle Strategy

First Fruits

SESSION THREE

first fruits

questions to think about

1. How might you have felt if you were one of the Israelites who had crossed the Jordan River into the Promised Land and had immediately encountered the fortified city of Jericho?

2. What are some of the intimidating, well-established, evil aspects of our society that Christians must confront if they follow God's calling and seek to bring His standards to bear on society?

3. Consider what is required to stand up and battle against the established evils of our society. In what ways are your feelings similar to or unlike what you imagine you would have felt as an Israelite facing Jericho?

43

---

44   Faith Lessons on the Promised Land

video notes

The City of Jericho

Rahab

God's Battle Strategy

First Fruits

PLANNING NOTES:

Group Discovery

20 minutes

If your group has seven or more members, use the **Video Highlights** with the entire group (5 minutes), then break into small groups of three to five to discuss the **Small Group Bible Discovery** (10 minutes). Then reassemble the group to discuss the key points discovered (5 minutes).

If your group has fewer than seven members, begin with the **Video Highlights** (5 minutes), then do one or more of the topics found in the **Small Group Bible Discovery** as a group (10 minutes). Finally, spend five minutes at the end discussing points that had an impact on participants.

Video Highlights (5 minutes)

Here you'll ask one or more of the following questions that directly relate to the video the participants have just seen.

Participant's Guide page 45.

Locate Jericho on the map of Israel on page 45 of your Participant's Guide.

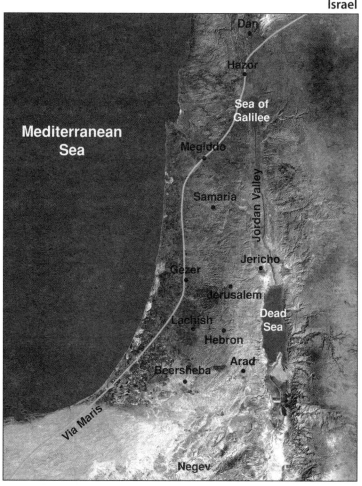

Session Three: First Fruits   45

video highlights

Locate Jericho on the map of Israel below.

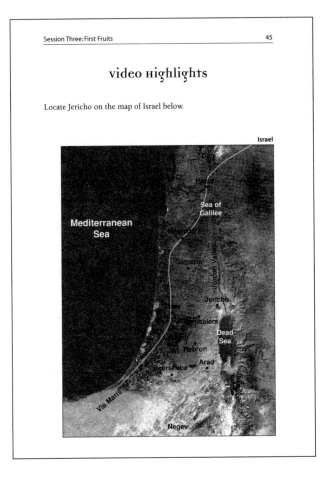

✏ 1.   Why was Jericho such a strategic city during ancient times?

Suggested Responses: was on the road linking the Via Maris and the King's Highway, was located near one of the few mountain passes where travelers from the east could enter Canaan, had a good source of water, was well-fortified, was located in a very defensible position, had the advantages of being a long-established city, etc.

✏ 2.   Were you surprised to learn that Rahab is listed in the genealogy of Jesus? Why or why not?

Suggested Responses: may vary a great deal, including the fact that biblical genealogies usually listed men only, that Rahab had been a prostitute in a pagan city, etc.

✏ 3.   In what ways did God clearly communicate that the battle for Jericho was His?

Suggested Responses: His angel appeared to Joshua and said so, the spies were protected, the battle plan seemed ridiculous—no one could defeat a city by parading around it; the battle itself was miraculous; the defeat of the city was complete; God's instructions afterward confirmed to whom the victory belonged, etc.

✏ 4.   How has your view of God's principle of "first fruits" changed as a result of seeing this video?

Suggested Responses: Allow participants to share their perspectives.

Small Group Bible Discovery (10 minutes)

Participant's Guide pages 47–56.

During this time, a group with fewer than seven participants will stay together. A group with seven or more participants will break into small groups and reassemble as a large group during the final five minutes. Assign each group one of the following topics. If you have more than five small groups, assign some topics to more than one group.

Let's break into groups of three to five—people sitting near you—and study some of the Bible passages and truths mentioned in the video.

Turn to pages 47–56 in your Participant's Guide. There you'll find five topics. You'll have ten minutes to read and discuss the topic I'll assign to you. Choose one person in your group to be a spokesperson for your group when we discuss these topics later.

Assign each group a topic.

I'll signal you when one minute is left.

46   Faith Lessons on the Promised Land

1. Why was Jericho such a strategic city during ancient times?

2. Were you surprised to learn that Rahab is listed in the genealogy of Jesus? Why or why not?

3. In what ways did God clearly communicate that the battle for Jericho was His?

4. How has your view of God's principle of "first fruits" changed as a result of seeing this video?

PLANNING NOTES:

After nine minutes, let participants know that they have one minute remaining. Then reassemble the entire group. After everyone is back together, begin asking one person from each small group to briefly share a key idea with the larger group. In some cases, you may not have time for every group to share their discoveries.

As time allows, let's briefly share the key ideas that your group discussed.

Topic A: Rahab—A Woman with an Incredible Story

1. What happened when Joshua sent two spies into Jericho? (See Joshua 2:1–7.)

    Suggested Responses: They immediately went into the house of Rahab, a prostitute, for lodging. The king of Jericho learned that spies were in the city and demanded that Rahab turn the men over to him, but Rahab claimed that the men had already left her house and urged the king's men to hurry and look for the spies elsewhere.

2. What did Rahab say to the foreign spies? (See Joshua 2:8–13.) Why did she risk so much to protect them?

    Suggested Responses: She knew the Lord had given the land to His people, that her people were afraid because they had heard about the Red Sea miracle and how the Israelites had destroyed the two kings of the Ammorites, that the Lord their God is God in heaven and on earth, and that she wanted the Israelites to be kind to her family because she had been kind to the spies. She risked everything because she had heard what God had done on behalf of His people and believed that the Israelites' God, not her people's gods, was "God in heaven above and on the earth below."

3. What did the spies promise to do for her? (See Joshua 2:14, 17–19.)

    Suggested Response: If she didn't reveal what they were doing and tied the scarlet cord in her window, the spies guaranteed her safety and the safety of any family members who remained in her house.

4. Why do you think God allowed the Israelites to spare the lives of Rahab and her family when Jericho was destroyed? (See Joshua 6:20–25.)

    Suggested Responses: He honored the promise the spies had made to her, what she had done to save their lives, and her faith in Him—the true God of heaven and earth.

5. What do you understand about the character of God when you read Matthew 1:1–7 and discover Rahab's name in the genealogy of Jesus?

    Suggested Responses: that God is forgiving of our sins and that He can use anyone, in spite of his or her evil past, to fulfill His plans.

small Group bible Discovery

Topic A: Rahab—A Woman with an Incredible Story

1. What happened when Joshua sent two spies into Jericho? (See Joshua 2:1–7.)

2. What did Rahab say to the foreign spies? (See Joshua 2:8–13.) Why did she risk so much to protect them?

3. What did the spies promise to do for her? (See Joshua 2:14, 17–19.)

4. Why do you think God allowed the Israelites to spare the lives of Rahab and her family when Jericho was destroyed? (See Joshua 6:20–25.)

5. What do you understand about the character of God when you read Matthew 1:1–7 and discover Rahab's name in the genealogy of Jesus?

Topic B: The People God Can Use

1. Look up each of the following passages and summarize what you discover about the people God has used to carry out His plans.

   a. Genesis 38:6–7, 11–19; Matthew 1:3a

   b. Joshua 2:1–15; 6:22–25; Matthew 1:5a

   c. Ruth 1:1–8, 14–16, 22; Matthew 1:5b

   d. 2 Samuel 11:1–5, 14–17; Matthew 1:6

PLANNING NOTES:

Topic B: The People God Can Use

1. Look up each of the following passages and summarize what you discover about the people God has used to carry out His plans.

    a. Genesis 38:6–7, 11–19; Matthew 1:3a

        Suggested Responses: Judah, who had not arranged for his widowed daughter-in-law to become pregnant and maintain his dead son's lineage, had sexual relations with her while thinking she was a prostitute. Nevertheless God chose Judah to be in the lineage of Jesus the Messiah.

    b. Joshua 2:1–15; 6:22–25; Matthew 1:5a

        Suggested Responses: Although Rahab was a prostitute in Jericho, she protected the two spies of Israel from the king of Jericho. Because of her faith in God and what she had done to save the spies' lives, she and her family were saved from death. She became the mother of Boaz, and God chose her to be in the lineage of Jesus the Messiah.

    c. Ruth 1:1–8, 14–16, 22; Matthew 1:5b

        Suggested Responses: Ruth, a pagan woman from Moab, married an Israelite man who had fled to Moab during a famine. After her husband died, she chose to follow the God of her husband and accompanied her widowed mother-in-law to Judah, where God had provided food for His people. As it turns out, God chose Ruth—a widow from a pagan culture—to be in the lineage of Jesus the Messiah.

    d. 2 Samuel 11:1–5, 14–17; Matthew 1:6

        Suggested Responses: David saw Bathsheba (Uriah's wife) bathing and summoned her to his palace, where they had sexual relations. When she became pregnant, David had Uriah murdered. Yet God chose David and Bathsheba (Solomon's mother) to be the Messiah's ancestors.

2. In light of their life stories, what is the significance of God choosing Rahab, Bathsheba, Tamar, and Ruth to be in Jesus' ancestral line?

    Suggested Responses: The fact that He gave these women a place of honor in the Messiah's genealogy, at a time when women were generally not included in biblical genealogies, demonstrates the completeness of His forgiveness of sin. It shows that He values all people who come to Him.

3. With these biblical accounts in mind, who else can you think of who came from a sinful past, chose a personal relationship with God through Jesus, and went on to become a powerful instrument in sharing the message of Jesus?

    Suggested Responses: will vary but may include such people as Nicky Cruz, St. Augustine, Charles Colson, etc.

5. What do you understand about the character of God when you read Matthew 1:1–7 and discover Rahab's name in the genealogy of Jesus?

Topic B: The People God Can Use

1. Look up each of the following passages and summarize what you discover about the people God has used to carry out His plans.

   a. Genesis 38:6–7, 11–19; Matthew 1:3a

   b. Joshua 2:1–15; 6:22–25; Matthew 1:5a

   c. Ruth 1:1–8, 14–16, 22; Matthew 1:5b

   d. 2 Samuel 11:1–5, 14–17; Matthew 1:6

2. In light of their life stories, what is the significance of God choosing Rahab, Bathsheba, Tamar, and Ruth to be in Jesus' ancestral line?

3. With these biblical accounts in mind, who else can you think of who came from a sinful past, chose a personal relationship with God through Jesus, and went on to become a powerful instrument in sharing the message of Jesus?

Topic C: God's Love of Holiness

The conquest of Canaan and the destruction of cities such as Jericho poses an ethical dilemma for many Bible readers. How could the God of love and mercy demand such merciless destruction of the inhabitants of the Promised Land? Although none of us can completely understand the sovereign God of the universe, the Bible reveals much about how seriously God views sin.

1. What kind of a world did God create from the chaos of water? (See Genesis 1–2, especially 1:2, 31.)

2. How did Adam and Eve—the crown of God's creation—respond toward God in the Garden of Eden? (See Genesis 3:1–12.)

PLANNING NOTES:

Topic C: God's Love of Holiness

The conquest of Canaan and the destruction of cities such as Jericho poses an ethical dilemma for many Bible readers. How could the God of love and mercy demand such merciless destruction of the inhabitants of the Promised Land? Although none of us can completely understand the sovereign God of the universe, the Bible reveals much about how seriously God views sin.

1. What kind of a world did God create from the chaos of water? (See Genesis 1–2, especially 1:2, 31.)

   Suggested Response: He created a beautiful, perfect world, and He was pleased with the goodness of His work.

2. How did Adam and Eve—the crown of God's creation—respond toward God in the Garden of Eden? (See Genesis 3:1–12.)

   Suggested Responses: They rebelled against their Creator; they refused to obey Him; they chose the way of evil rather than His way; they fled from fellowship with Him; etc.

3. What has God always wanted His people to be? (See Joshua 24:19–23; Leviticus 11:44; 1 Peter 1:15; 2:9.)

   Suggested Response: God's people have always been set apart for God, called to be holy as He is holy.

4. What do each of the following passages reveal about how God views sin?

Numbers 15:32–40	God takes disobedience of His laws very seriously. He wants His people to be holy and had a man stoned for working on the Sabbath.
Exodus 19:5–6	God promised to make Israel His treasured possession—a holy nation—if they obeyed Him fully.
Exodus 32:1, 7–14, 31–35	While Moses was on Mount Sinai, the people worshiped a golden calf, which so angered God that He threatened to destroy them. Moses interceded for them, so God spared their lives, but God did not let their sin go unpunished.
1 Corinthians 6:18–20	As God's people, we have been bought with a price, and our bodies are temples of the Holy Spirit. Therefore we are to be sexually pure and to honor God with our bodies.

5. In contrast to the Israelites, who were called to be holy before God, what were the pagan inhabitants of Canaan like? (See Leviticus 18:1–5, 24–30; Deuteronomy 18:9–13.)

   Suggested Responses: walked in their own ways, not the ways of God; rejected God, were so sinful that they had defiled the land itself; engaged in abominable, perverse worship of the fertility gods of the Near East; indulged in the occult; were an affront to a holy God; etc.

2. In light of their life stories, what is the significance of God choosing Rahab, Bathsheba, Tamar, and Ruth to be in Jesus' ancestral line?

3. With these biblical accounts in mind, who else can you think of who came from a sinful past, chose a personal relationship with God through Jesus, and went on to become a powerful instrument in sharing the message of Jesus?

Topic C: God's Love of Holiness

The conquest of Canaan and the destruction of cities such as Jericho poses an ethical dilemma for many Bible readers. How could the God of love and mercy demand such merciless destruction of the inhabitants of the Promised Land? Although none of us can completely understand the sovereign God of the universe, the Bible reveals much about how seriously God views sin.

1. What kind of a world did God create from the chaos of water? (See Genesis 1–2, especially 1:2, 31.)

2. How did Adam and Eve—the crown of God's creation—respond toward God in the Garden of Eden? (See Genesis 3:1–12.)

3. What has God always wanted His people to be? (See Joshua 24:19–23; Leviticus 11:44; 1 Peter 1:15; 2:9.)

4. What do each of the following passages reveal about how God views sin?

Numbers 15:32–40	
Exodus 19:5–6	
Exodus 32:1, 7–14, 31–35	
1 Corinthians 6:18–20	

5. In contrast to the Israelites, who were called to be holy before God, what were the pagan inhabitants of Canaan like? (See Leviticus 18:1–5, 24–30; Deuteronomy 18:9–13.)

PLANNING NOTES:

Topic D: When God's Judgment Falls

1. As the Israelites prepared to battle the pagan nations in the Promised Land, what instructions did God give them concerning their attacks on cities such as Jericho, and why? (See Deuteronomy 20:16–18; Joshua 6:16–18, 21–24.)

   Suggested Responses: They were to kill every living thing in every city they captured in the Promised Land. God knew that if they didn't do this, the idol-worshiping Canaanites would teach the Israelites to do the same evil things they did in worshiping their gods, and He didn't want His people to sin.

2. What accompanied the Israelites as they marched around Jericho? Why? (See Joshua 6:6–9.)

   Suggested Responses: They carried the ark of the covenant, the representation of God's presence among them. By doing so, the Israelites were acknowledging God to be their God, declaring that He went before them into battle, and affirming their faith in Him.

DATA FILE

The Judgment of God

The judgment of God (called *cherem* in Hebrew) is translated "totally devoted to God" or "utterly destroyed." In modern English, we might say "damned." Only such total judgment could remove the pollution of sin so that God's creation would again honor Him.

The Bible provides several examples of God's *cherem* falling on sinful people:

- Genesis 6–8—God flooded the whole earth to wash away a perverse human race.
- Genesis 19—God poured fire and brimstone on the evil cities of Sodom and Gomorrah.
- Numbers 16—Because they defied Him, God destroyed Korah, Dathan, Abiram, and their followers, as well as all of their family members and belongings.

The conquest of Canaan was another step in God's plan to reclaim His world. Only the total destruction of the sinful Canaanites would make the land fit for God's people to serve Him and enable them to become a blessing to all nations so that the world would know that Yahweh is God. To bring about His judgment and restoration, God chose as His instruments the same creatures who had sinned against Him.

Topic D: When God's Judgment Falls

1. As the Israelites prepared to battle the pagan nations in the Promised Land, what instructions did God give them concerning their attacks on cities such as Jericho, and why? (See Deuteronomy 20:16–18; Joshua 6:16–18, 21–24.)

DATA FILE

The Judgment of God

The judgment of God (called *cherem* in Hebrew) is translated "totally devoted to God" or "utterly destroyed." In modern English, we might say "damned." Only such total judgment could remove the pollution of sin so that God's creation would again honor Him.

The Bible provides several examples of God's *cherem* falling on sinful people:

- Genesis 6–8—God flooded the whole earth to wash away a perverse human race.
- Genesis 19—God poured fire and brimstone on the evil cities of Sodom and Gomorrah.
- Numbers 16—Because they defied Him, God destroyed Korah, Dathan, Abiram, and their followers, as well as all of their family members and belongings.

The conquest of Canaan was another step in God's plan to reclaim His world. Only the total destruction of the sinful Canaanites would make the land fit for God's people to serve Him and enable them to become a blessing to all nations so that the world would know that Yahweh is God. To bring about His judgment and restoration, God chose as His instruments the same creatures who had sinned against Him.

2. What accompanied the Israelites as they marched around Jericho? Why? (See Joshua 6:6–9.)

3. What similarities do you note between Joshua 6:15–16, 20 and 1 Thessalonians 4:16?

4. Look up the following verses and describe God's response to and judgment of sin.

Genesis 6:5–9, 13–14, 17–18; 7:23	
Genesis 18:20–33; 19:1, 12–13, 24–25	
Numbers 16:1–11, 20–35	
Numbers 25:1–9	
Revelation 20:7–10	

5. Contrast God's judgment of sin with what we read in John 3:16 and 1 John 1:9.

PLANNING NOTES:

✏ 3.   What similarities do you note between Joshua 6:15–16, 20 and 1 Thessalonians 4:16?

Suggested Response: Just as the Israelites announced God's judgment of Jericho with their trumpet blast and shouts, during the final judgment the Lord will come down from heaven with a loud command, with the voice of the archangel and the trumpet call of God.

✏ 4.   Look up the following verses and describe God's response to and judgment of sin.

Genesis 6:5–9, 13–14, 17–18; 7:23	God was so grieved by the evil of man that He was sorry He had made man. Only Noah was righteous, so God sent a great flood that killed every living thing that drew breath and was not preserved with Noah in the ark.
Genesis 18:20–33; 19:1, 12–13, 24–25	The sins of Sodom and Gomorrah were grave. After Abraham pleaded with God on behalf of the cities, God spared righteous Lot and his family but destroyed all living things in the cities— and even the surrounding vegetation.
Numbers 16:1–11, 20–35	Korah, Dathan, and Abiram rebelled against Moses (God's chosen leader), as did 250 other well-known community leaders. God was ready to destroy the entire congregation, but Moses and Aaron pled on behalf of the people. God then limited His destruction to the men involved, their families, and their possessions.
Numbers 25:1–9	Israelite men began committing sexual immorality with Moabite women, which led to the Israelites' worship of false gods. God caused a plague to strike down the Israelites, and it killed 24,000 people before Phinehas took action against the sin and checked the plague.
Revelation 20:7–10	Satan, the deceiver who led people into evil, will be thrown into the "lake of burning sulfur" where he will be tormented forever and ever.

✏ 5.   Contrast God's judgment of sin with what we read in John 3:16 and 1 John 1:9.

Suggested Responses: God hates sin more than we can imagine, but He also sent His beloved Son—the Messiah—to die for our sins. God is eager to forgive our sins and allow us to escape the final judgment if we put our personal faith in Jesus and seek forgiveness and cleansing through His death on the cross.

2. What accompanied the Israelites as they marched around Jericho? Why? (See Joshua 6:6–9.)

3. What similarities do you note between Joshua 6:15–16, 20 and 1 Thessalonians 4:16?

4. Look up the following verses and describe God's response to and judgment of sin.

Genesis 6:5–9, 13–14, 17–18; 7:23	
Genesis 18:20–33; 19:1, 12–13, 24–25	
Numbers 16:1–11, 20–35	
Numbers 25:1–9	
Revelation 20:7–10	

5. Contrast God's judgment of sin with what we read in John 3:16 and 1 John 1:9.

PLANNING NOTES:

DATA FILE

The Holy, the Common, and the Abominable

The Old Testament view of sin and judgment produced a concept of reality divided into three parts: the holy, the common, and the abominable (unclean).

The Holy

Anything devoted to Yahweh or used in His service was considered holy. God made some things, such as the Sabbath, holy. Some things became holy (such as first fruits) because they were offered to God in service. Once something had been given to God, it was His alone.

The worst kind of sin was to use something holy for one's personal benefit. Jericho had been given to God, so it was not to be inhabited again. Israel, as a nation, had been set apart to serve God, so it could not worship anyone or anything else. And according to the New Testament, every Christian is holy, set apart to serve God. So we cannot and must not serve any other person, idea, or thing. Every part of our lives should be dedicated to serving the Lord—including our occupations, families, and recreation. Nothing is to be done for our benefit alone. To do so is to place ourselves under His judgment.

The Common

In the Old Testament, things that belonged to the people were considered common: household possessions, animals, land, etc. These things were to be used in godly ways, but they were under the stewardship of the people who owned them. In the New Testament, however, the holy and common were joined. Everything, even the mundane, is now to be used in God's service.

The prophet Zechariah said that when the Messiah returns, even the bowls used in family cooking will be as sacred as those used in temple worship. "And on that day there will no longer be a Canaanite in the house of the Lord Almighty" (Zechariah 14:20–21). That is the story of Jericho. The Canaanites living there had polluted God's land and had to be removed by His judgment. Then the holy people of God could begin to find ways to serve Him in every part of their lives.

The Abominable

God detests abominations—anything associated with the worship of other gods and any behavior that perverts the lifestyle God intended human beings to live. Leviticus 18 contains a list of unlawful behaviors (e.g., incest, adultery, homosexuality, bestiality). As He demonstrated by sending the Great Flood, the judgment on Sodom and Gomorrah, and various judgments on the Israelites, God will judge people who practice these behaviors.

DATA FILE

The Holy, the Common, and the Abominable

The Old Testament view of sin and judgment produced a concept of reality divided into three parts: the holy, the common, and the abominable (unclean).

The Holy

Anything devoted to Yahweh or used in His service was considered holy. God made some things, such as the Sabbath, holy. Some things became holy (such as first fruits) because they were offered to God in service. Once something had been given to God, it was His alone.

The worst kind of sin was to use something holy for one's personal benefit. Jericho had been given to God, so it was not to be inhabited again. Israel, as a nation, had been set apart to serve God, so it could not worship anyone or anything else. And according to the New Testament, every Christian is holy, set apart to serve God. So we cannot and must not serve any other person, idea, or thing. Every part of our lives should be dedicated to serving the Lord—including our occupations, families, and recreation. Nothing is to be done for our benefit alone. To do so is to place ourselves under His judgment.

The Common

In the Old Testament, things that belonged to the people were considered common: household possessions, animals, land, etc. These things were to be used in godly ways, but they were under the stewardship of the people who owned them. In the New Testament, however, the holy and common were joined. Everything, even mundane things, is now to be used in God's service.

The prophet Zechariah said that when the Messiah returns, even the bowls used in family cooking will be as sacred as those used in temple worship. "And on that day there will no longer be a Canaanite in the house of the Lord Almighty" (Zechariah 14:20–21). That is the story of Jericho. The Canaanites living there had polluted God's land and had to be removed by His judgment. Then the holy people of God could begin to find ways to serve Him in every part of their lives.

(continued on page 54)

(continued from page 53)

The Abominable

God detests abominations—anything associated with the worship of other gods and any behavior that perverts the lifestyle God intended human beings to live. Leviticus 18 contains a list of unlawful behaviors (e.g., incest, adultery, homosexuality, bestiality). As He demonstrated by sending the Great Flood, the judgment on Sodom and Gomorrah, and various judgments on the Israelites, God will judge people who practice these behaviors.

Topic E: Set Apart for God

The principle of "first fruits" reinforces the truth that God is the giver of everything. To give God the first fruits is an act of faith that expresses trust in God to provide the rest. To take the first fruits for ourselves is to deny God's ownership of our blessings and to fail to live by faith.

1. What was God's desire concerning the first portion of whatever blessings He gave to Israel? (Read Leviticus 23:9–14.)

2. How did this principle apply to the spoils of Jericho, the first city that God gave to Israel? (Read Joshua 6:19, 26.)

PLANNING NOTES:

Topic E: Set Apart for God

The principle of "first fruits" reinforces the truth that God is the giver of everything. To give God the first fruits is an act of faith that expresses trust in God to provide the rest. To take the first fruits for ourselves is to deny God's ownership of our blessings and to fail to live by faith.

1. What was God's desire concerning the first portion of whatever blessings He gave to Israel? (Read Leviticus 23:9–14.)

   Suggested Response: God desired that the Israelites who entered the Promised Land give Him a portion of the first crops harvested each year.

2. How did this principle apply to the spoils of Jericho, the first city that God gave to Israel? (Read Joshua 6:19, 26.)

   Suggested Responses: After Jericho was captured, God desired that all of the silver, gold, bronze, and iron items be given to Him for His treasury, and, through Joshua, commanded that the city not be rebuilt.

3. Instead of obeying God and giving Him the first fruits of the Canaanites' wealth, what did one of the Israelites do? What happened as a consequence? (See Joshua 7:1–12, 24–26.)

   Suggested Responses: Achan took some of the valuable items captured in Jericho for himself instead of giving them to God. So God allowed the small army of Ai to rout the Israelite soldiers and kill about thirty-six of them. Joshua—with prophetic guidance from God—pointed out who had committed the sin. Then the Israelites killed Achan, his family, and his animals, and burned the remains.

WHAT IS A *MEZUZAH?*

Attached to the doorpost of every religious Jewish home is a small container called a *mezuzah* that holds a rolled parchment inscribed with Bible verses (the text of Deuteronomy 4:4–9; 11:13–21). A Jewish person entering the home touches the *mezuzah* and then kisses his or her fingers as an expression of devotion to the verses it contains. The Jews also customarily say, "May God protect my going out and coming in, now and forever."

The Tradition Behind It

Jewish scholars base the custom of the *mezuzah* on Deuteronomy 6:6, 9: "These commandments that I give you today are to be upon your hearts. . . . Write them on the doorframes of your houses and on your gates." The physical presence of a copy of the Deuteronomy commandments provided an excellent reminder of God's desires for His people.

Jericho's Ruins Were Like a Mezuzah

The main, eastern gate or doorway to the Promised Land is the mountain pass guarded by Jericho. Appropriately, God commanded that the city's ruins be left as a testimony, like a *mezuzah,* that the land belonged to Him and that His people who lived in it sought to serve Him. God wanted His mark of ownership to remain on the land as a reminder that its inhabitants must live by His laws.

(continued from page 53)

The Abominable

God detests abominations—anything associated with the worship of other gods and any behavior that perverts the lifestyle God intended human beings to live. Leviticus 18 contains a list of unlawful behaviors (e.g., incest, adultery, homosexuality, bestiality). As He demonstrated by sending the Great Flood, the judgment on Sodom and Gomorrah, and various judgments on the Israelites, God will judge people who practice these behaviors.

Topic E: Set Apart for God

The principle of "first fruits" reinforces the truth that God is the giver of everything. To give God the first fruits is an act of faith that expresses trust in God to provide the rest. To take the first fruits for ourselves is to deny God's ownership of our blessings and to fail to live by faith.

1. What was God's desire concerning the first portion of whatever blessings He gave to Israel? (Read Leviticus 23:9–14.)

2. How did this principle apply to the spoils of Jericho, the first city that God gave to Israel? (Read Joshua 6:19, 26.)

3. Instead of obeying God and giving Him the first fruits of the Canaanites' wealth, what did one of the Israelites do? What happened as a consequence? (See Joshua 7:1–12, 24–26.)

WHAT IS A *MEZUZAH*?

Attached to the doorpost of every religious Jewish home is a small container called a *mezuzah* that holds a rolled parchment inscribed with Bible verses (the text of Deuteronomy 4:4–9; 11:13–21). A Jewish person entering the home touches the *mezuzah* and then kisses his or her fingers as an expression of devotion to the verses it contains. The Jews also customarily say, "May God protect my going out and coming in, now and forever."

The Tradition Behind It

Jewish scholars base the custom of the *mezuzah* on Deuteronomy 6:6, 9: "These commandments that I give you today are to be upon your hearts. . . . Write them on the doorframes of your houses and on your gates." The physical presence of a copy of the Deuteronomy commandments provided an excellent reminder of God's desires for His people.

Jericho's Ruins Were Like a Mezuzah

The main, eastern gate or doorway to the Promised Land is the mountain pass guarded by Jericho. Appropriately, God commanded that the city's ruins be left as a testimony, like a *mezuzah*, that the land belonged to Him and that His people who lived in it sought to serve Him. God wanted His mark of ownership to remain on the land as a reminder that its inhabitants must live by His laws.

✏ 4. As the Israelites watched God's judgment focusing on the tribes, then the clans of Judah, and finally on Achan's family itself (Joshua 7:13–18), what effect do you think that process had on the people? What did God's punishment (Joshua 7:24–25) communicate about God's tolerance of sin?

Suggested Responses: The people may have become afraid of God's judgment, realized that God knew everything they did and thought, and become angry at the person who had disobeyed God and brought His judgment on them. Certainly the punishment communicated that God would not tolerate sin among His people.

✏ 5. When you read about what happened to Hiel of Bethel, are you surprised? Why or why not? (See Joshua 6:26–27 and 1 Kings 16:29–34.)

Suggested Responses: may vary, but God had foretold how the man who rebuilt Jericho would be punished, so it shouldn't surprise us that God fulfilled His promise.

✏ 6. What were the ruins of Jericho to communicate to all future generations? (See Joshua 6:20–21, 24.)

Suggested Responses: to be a testimony to all future generations of God's ownership of the Israelites and their willingness to live by faith in Him. The ruins, like a *mezuzah*, reminded everyone who entered Israel that it was God's land inhabited by God's people. God wanted His mark of ownership to remain on the land as a reminder that its inhabitants must live by His law.

faith Lesson

10 minutes

Time for Reflection (5 minutes)

It's time for each of us to think quietly about how we can apply what we've learned today. On pages 57–58 of your Participant's Guide, you'll find a passage of Scripture. Let's each read this passage silently and take the next few minutes to consider some of the questions that follow.

Please do not talk during this time. It's a time when we all can reflect on today's lesson and how it applies to our lives.

The Scripture passage and questions are reproduced in their entirety in the Participant's Guide on pages 57–58.

Now Jericho was tightly shut up because of the Israelites. No one went out and no one came in.

Then the LORD said to Joshua, "See, I have delivered Jericho into your hands, along with its king and its fighting men. March around the city once with all the armed men. Do this for six days. Have seven priests carry trumpets of rams' horns in front of the ark. On the seventh day, march around the city seven times, with the priests blowing the trumpets. When you hear them sound a long blast on the trumpets, have all the people give a loud

4. As the Israelites watched God's judgment focusing on the tribes, then the clans of Judah, and finally on Achan's family itself (Joshua 7:13–18), what effect do you think that process had on the people? What did God's punishment (Joshua 7:24–25) communicate about God's tolerance of sin?

5. When you read about what happened to Hiel of Bethel, are you surprised? Why or why not? (See Joshua 6:26–27 and 1 Kings 16:29–34.)

6. What were the ruins of Jericho to communicate to all future generations? (See Joshua 6:20–21, 24.)

ꜰaith Lesson

Time for Reflection

Read the following passage of Scripture silently and take the next few minutes to consider how God uses people who are committed to Him to accomplish His purposes.

> Now Jericho was tightly shut up because of the Israelites. No one went out and no one came in.
>
> Then the LORD said to Joshua, "See, I have delivered Jericho into your hands, along with its king and its fighting men. March around the city once with all the armed men. Do this for six days. Have seven priests carry trumpets of rams' horns in front of the ark. On the seventh day, march around the city seven times, with the priests blowing the trumpets. When you hear them sound a long blast on the trumpets, have all the people give a loud shout; then the wall of the city will collapse and the people will go up, every man straight in."
>
> . . . On the seventh day, they got up at daybreak and marched around the city seven times in the same manner, except that on that day they circled the city seven times. The seventh time around, when the priests sounded the trumpet blast, Joshua commanded the people, "Shout! For the LORD has given you the city! The city and all that is in it are to be devoted to the LORD. Only Rahab the prostitute and all who are with her in her house shall be spared, because she hid the spies we sent. But keep away from the devoted things, so that you will not bring about your own destruction by taking any of them. Otherwise you will make the camp of Israel liable to destruction and bring trouble on it. All the silver and gold and the articles of bronze and iron are sacred to the LORD and must go into his treasury."
>
> When the trumpets sounded, the people shouted, and at the sound of the trumpet, when the people gave a loud shout, the wall collapsed; so every man charged straight in, and they took the city.

PLANNING NOTES:

shout; then the wall of the city will collapse and the people will go up, every man straight in."

... On the seventh day, they got up at daybreak and marched around the city seven times in the same manner, except that on that day they circled the city seven times. The seventh time around, when the priests sounded the trumpet blast, Joshua commanded the people, "Shout! For the LORD has given you the city! The city and all that is in it are to be devoted to the LORD. Only Rahab the prostitute and all who are with her in her house shall be spared, because she hid the spies we sent. But keep away from the devoted things, so that you will not bring about your own destruction by taking any of them. Otherwise you will make the camp of Israel liable to destruction and bring trouble on it. All the silver and gold and the articles of bronze and iron are sacred to the LORD and must go into his treasury."

When the trumpets sounded, the people shouted, and at the sound of the trumpet, when the people gave a loud shout, the wall collapsed; so every man charged straight in, and they took the city. They devoted the city to the LORD and destroyed with the sword every living thing in it—men and women, young and old, cattle, sheep and donkeys.

JOSHUA 6:1–5, 15–21

1. When the Israelites marched around Jericho, the ark of the covenant went with them. Why is it important to remember that God is with you as you seek to live by His truths and reveal Him to a culture that rejects Him?

2. What is encouraging to you about the fact that God used sinful people in spite of their pasts and even chose them to be in the lineage of the Messiah?

3. If you are a follower of Jesus, you are holy and "set apart" for God. What does the fact that you are holy tell you about the lifestyle you should lead? What changes do you need to make in order to live out your calling?

> As soon as participants have spent five minutes reflecting on the above questions, get the entire group's attention and move to the next section.

Action Points (5 minutes)

> The following points are reproduced on pages 59–60 of the Participant's Guide:

Now it's time to wrap up our session.

> Give participants a moment to transition from their thoughtfulness to giving you their full attention.

faith lesson

Time for Reflection

Read the following passage of Scripture silently and take the next few minutes to consider how God uses people who are committed to Him to accomplish His purposes.

> Now Jericho was tightly shut up because of the Israelites. No one went out and no one came in.
>
> Then the LORD said to Joshua, "See, I have delivered Jericho into your hands, along with its king and its fighting men. March around the city once with all the armed men. Do this for six days. Have seven priests carry trumpets of rams' horns in front of the ark. On the seventh day, march around the city seven times, with the priests blowing the trumpets. When you hear them sound a long blast on the trumpets, have all the people give a loud shout; then the wall of the city will collapse and the people will go up, every man straight in."
>
> . . . On the seventh day, they got up at daybreak and marched around the city seven times in the same manner, except that on that day they circled the city seven times. The seventh time around, when the priests sounded the trumpet blast, Joshua commanded the people, "Shout! For the LORD has given you the city! The city and all that is in it are to be devoted to the LORD. Only Rahab the prostitute and all who are with her in her house shall be spared, because she hid the spies we sent. But keep away from the devoted things, so that you will not bring about your own destruction by taking any of them. Otherwise you will make the camp of Israel liable to destruction and bring trouble on it. All the silver and gold and the articles of bronze and iron are sacred to the LORD and must go into his treasury."
>
> When the trumpets sounded, the people shouted, and at the sound of the trumpet, when the people gave a loud shout, the wall collapsed; so every man charged straight in, and they took the city.

> They devoted the city to the LORD and destroyed with the sword every living thing in it—men and women, young and old, cattle, sheep and donkeys.
>
> JOSHUA 6:1–5, 15–21

1. When the Israelites marched around Jericho, the ark of the covenant went with them. Why is it important to remember that God is with you as you seek to live by His truths and reveal Him to a culture that rejects Him?

2. What is encouraging to you about the fact that God used sinful people in spite of their pasts and even chose them to be in the lineage of the Messiah?

3. If you are a follower of Jesus, you are holy and "set apart" for God. What does the fact that you are holy tell you about the lifestyle you should lead? What changes do you need to make in order to live out your calling?

PLANNING NOTES:

I'd like to take a moment to summarize the key points we explored. After I have reviewed each point, I will give you a moment to jot down an action step (or steps) that you will commit to this week as a result of what you have learned today.

> Read each point and pause for a minute or so in order for participants to consider and write out their commitment.

1. *As the Israelites took possession of the Promised Land, God clearly demonstrated that the battle against its pagan inhabitants was His battle, not theirs.*

   Likewise, as we seek to bring God's value system into our culture and to confront that which is contrary to God's way, we need to remember that the battle is the Lord's. He is the one who seeks to reclaim the world He created, and we are His instruments in that process.

   As you confront the secular world's value system, which battles will you face?

   In what ways can you let them be God's battles, not yours?

2. *God's people are to follow the Old Testament principle of "first fruits," meaning we are to offer God the first part of what we receive as our provision.* By doing so, we acknowledge that God is the source of our provision and that we trust Him to continue to provide for us.

   If we give ourselves to God as His holy, "set-apart" people, He will take care of the rest! But if we use what has been set apart for God's use to benefit ourselves, we break the first-fruits principle. God does not provide for us so that we can honor ourselves. God gives us what we have—money, time, talents, etc.—so that He can use us as agents in His service.

   When you give God the first portion of the blessings He gives you, what are you demonstrating—to yourself and to a watching world?

   What has God provided for you to use in His service? In what ways might you be taking back God's first fruits in regard to your talents, your financial resources, your occupation, etc.?

closing prayer

I minute

Dear Lord, thank You for setting us apart for You. Help us to identify and avoid unholy things. How wonderful it is that Your standards for sin never change, and yet You love us so much and sent Your Son to die for our sins so that we might have eternal life with You. Amen.

Action Points

After you have reviewed the key points of this lesson, take a moment to jot down an action step (or steps) that you will commit to this week as a result of what you have learned today.

1. *As the Israelites took possession of the Promised Land, God clearly demonstrated that the battle against its pagan inhabitants was His battle, not theirs.*

   Likewise, as we seek to bring God's value system into our culture and to confront that which is contrary to God's way, we need to remember that the battle is the Lord's. He is the one who seeks to reclaim the world He created, and we are His instruments in that process.

   As you confront the secular world's value system, which battles will you face?

   In what ways can you let them be God's battles, not yours?

2. *God's people are to follow the Old Testament principle of "first fruits," meaning we are to offer God the first part of what we receive as our provision.* By doing so, we acknowledge that God is the source of our provision and that we trust Him to continue to provide for us.

   If we give ourselves to God as His holy, "set-apart" people, He will take care of the rest! But if we use what has been set apart for God's use to benefit ourselves, we break the first-fruits principle. God does not provide for us so that we can honor ourselves. God gives us what we have—

money, time, talents, etc.—so that He can use us as agents in His service.

When you give God the first portion of the blessings He gives you, what are you demonstrating—to yourself and to a watching world?

What has God provided for you to use in His service? In what ways might you be taking back God's first fruits in regard to your talents, your financial resources, your occupation, etc.?

PLANNING NOTES:

confronting evil

Before You Lead

Synopsis

During the time of the judges in ancient Israel, the sophisticated and powerful Philistines lived on the coastal plain by the Mediterranean Sea. The Israelites, who were far less advanced than the Philistines, lived in the Shephelah (the low foothills) and the Judea Mountains to the east.

Several broad valleys extended up from the coastal plain through the Shephelah and some distance into the mountains. These valleys became the crossroads of commerce and culture in the ancient world. They were the means by which trade routes could cross the mountains, linking the major powers of Egypt and Rome with the empires of Persia, Babylon, and Assyria. They were also the places where the opposing cultures of the Philistines and Israelites clashed as each sought to control this strategic region. Whoever controlled the foothills held the upper hand and could dominate the relationship between the two peoples.

Built by the people of the coastal plain, the city of Beth Shemesh was one of several cities in the valleys that extended into the Shephelah. It stood like a guardhouse over the Sorek Valley, where fierce fighting between the Philistines and the Israelites often took place. God had given this region in the Shephelah and part of the coastal plain to the small tribe of Dan as its inheritance. However, the tribe of Dan never drove out the Philistines, which created serious problems for God's people.

The Philistines worshiped such fertility gods as Dagon, the god of grain; his mistress Ashtoreth, who was associated with war and fertility; and Baal-Zebul, thought to be the son of Dagon. Worship of these gods was so immoral and abhorrent that the Israelites changed the name of Baal-Zebul to Baal-Zebub, which meant "lord of the flies." Jesus later referred to the devil as Beelzebub, which demonstrates how evil the Philistine religion was (Matthew 12:24–28). Unfortunately, the Israelites became attracted to the Philistines' lifestyle, culture, and superior technology and over time drew away from God. As punishment, God "delivered them into the hands of the Philistines for forty years" (Judges 13:1).

But God didn't abandon His people. He sent an angel to a childless couple from the tribe of Dan and said, in effect, "You're going to have a child. Now see to it that he becomes a Nazirite." A Nazirite was set apart from his culture. He didn't drink wine, the common drink. Unlike everyone else, he didn't cut his hair. He didn't touch anything dead, so he didn't eat meat. When God's people saw a Nazirite's unique lifestyle, they were reminded of what it meant to be set apart for God, to be different from the surrounding, ungodly culture.

God blessed Samson, the couple's son. After God's Spirit stirred inside him, Samson began confronting the evil Philistine culture. He used foxes to burn up huge wheat fields, carried the city gates of Gaza about forty-five miles to Hebron, and killed many Philistine soldiers. As long as he remained dedicated to God's values, Samson was effective in doing what God had called him to do.

But over time, Samson compromised more and more with the Philistines' value system and became less effective. He killed a lion with his bare hands—thus touching a dead body. He drank wine at his wedding party. And he committed sexual sin with Delilah, which led to his hair being cut. Consequently, his mission, walk with God, and physical body became weak. He lost spiritual and physical power.

Ray then shares how the Philistines later invaded the Israelites' turf in the mountains, thus jeopardizing God's plan of salvation. The Israelites, who had not been willing to confront the ungodly culture of the Philistines, had failed to live out their distinctiveness. They were in serious trouble, and in a last-ditch effort to regain God's power, Eli—the high priest—sent the ark of the covenant into battle. The Philistines captured the ark, but it brought them great trouble so they returned it (along with gifts of gold) to the Israelites. The Israelites then rejoiced greatly. They offered a sacrifice to God and left a standing stone to mark the spot where God's presence had been returned to them.

Key Points of This Lesson

1. *As God's people, we—like Samson and the tribe of Dan—are called to be part of the confrontation between God and the ungodliness of the world.* Our calling is to live on the front lines—in our equivalent of the Shephelah, the place where opposing values clash—in order to confront secular values and influence the world for God. But we can only live out a God-centered lifestyle if we refuse to adopt the ungodly values of our culture. Thus we are to remain distinct from the world's culture, not to compromise with it.

2. *When God calls us to accomplish a specific task, it is essential that we complete it fully.* If we don't, then we—like the tribe of Dan that failed to chase the Philistines out of the land God had provided for His people—jeopardize the whole mission. But when we place all aspects of our lives under the dominion of God's value system and live in close relationship with Him, God will work through us! We can have a powerful impact. We can be like standing stones that represent God and His power to our culture.

Session Outline (54 minutes)

I. **Introduction** (4 minutes)

Welcome

What's to Come

Questions to Think About

II. **Show Video "Confronting Evil"** (28 minutes)

III. **Group Discovery** (15 minutes)

Video Highlights

Small Group Bible Discovery

IV. **Faith Lesson** (6 minutes)

Time for Reflection

Action Points

V. **Closing Prayer** (1 minute)

Materials

No additional materials are needed for this session. Simply view the video prior to leading the session so you are familiar with its main points.

PLANNING NOTES:

confronting evil

introduction

Welcome

> Assemble the participants together. Welcome them to session four of *Faith Lessons on the Promised Land.*

What's to Come

When God gave the Promised Land to the Israelites, He commanded them to possess the land completely—to confront and remove the pagan cultures, to keep themselves separate from ungodly influences, and to influence the world for Him. But instead of driving out the Philistines from the land God had provided, the tribe of Dan allowed the Philistines to remain in power. Samson, whom God chose to reduce the Philistines' grip over Israel, also compromised himself—with serious consequences. In this session, we will see how vitally important it is to confront evil in our culture and to fully complete the mission God has called us to accomplish.

Questions to Think About

> *Participant's Guide page 61.*

Before we begin the video, let's consider several questions that will prepare us to consider the importance of the mission to which God has called us.

> Ask each question and solicit a few responses from group members.

✎ 1. When you hear the word "Philistine," which images come to mind?

Suggested Responses: Goliath, the enemies of Israel, people who worshiped false gods, an ancient civilization, cruelty, etc.

✎ 2. Even though God clearly tells His people that the values and lifestyle of the world's culture—whether it is the world of the Israelites or our world today—are sinful, we still find ourselves being drawn to them. Why is that?

Suggested Responses: Sin promises pleasure, and Satan tempts us with it. We are surrounded by ungodly values—even bombarded by them. And it's tough to confront sin because that puts us in conflict with people and makes us stand out as "different."

SESSION FOUR

confronting evil

questions to think about

1. When you hear the word "Philistine," which images come to mind?

2. Even though God clearly tells His people that the values and lifestyle of the world's culture—whether it is the world of the Israelites or our world today—are sinful, we still find ourselves being drawn to them. Why is that?

3. What can happen when we seek to follow God in most areas of our lives but have a few areas that are not committed to Him?

4. What is the result of compromising with a world that doesn't live according to God's values?

61

PLANNING NOTES:

✏ 3.   What can happen when we seek to follow God in most areas of our lives but have a few areas that are not committed to Him?

Suggested Responses: The areas in which we don't allow God to have control will cause problems for us; sin will grow in those areas and influence other parts of our lives; we will not have as strong a witness to the secular world; we may be unable to do what God wants us to do; etc.

✏ 4.   What is the result of compromising with a world that doesn't live according to God's values?

Suggested Responses: We lose our distinctiveness; we don't stand out as God's people; we become less effective in helping the world discover that God is the one true God; we can lose sight of our purpose; we can even compromise our faith; etc.

Let's keep these ideas in mind as we view the video.

video presentation

≥8 minutes

| *Participant's Guide page 62.* |

On page 62 of your Participant's Guide, you will find a space in which to take notes on key points as we watch this video.

Leader's Video Observations

The Philistines—the People, the Land

The Importance of Fulfilling God's Calling

Samson—His Calling, His Failing

The Consequences of Compromise

confronting evil

questions to think about

1. When you hear the word "Philistine," which images come to mind?

2. Even though God clearly tells His people that the values and lifestyle of the world's culture—whether it is the world of the Israelites or our world today—are sinful, we still find ourselves being drawn to them. Why is that?

3. What can happen when we seek to follow God in most areas of our lives but have a few areas that are not committed to Him?

4. What is the result of compromising with a world that doesn't live according to God's values?

61

video notes

The Philistines—the People, the Land

The Importance of Fulfilling God's Calling

Samson—His Calling, His Failing

The Consequences of Compromise

PLANNING NOTES:

Group Discovery

15 minutes

> If your group has seven or more members, use the **Video Highlights** with the entire group (5 minutes), then break into small groups of three to five to discuss the **Small Group Bible Discovery** (6 minutes). Then reassemble the group to discuss the key points discovered (4 minutes).
>
> If your group has fewer than seven members, begin with the **Video Highlights** (5 minutes), then do one or more of the topics found in the **Small Group Bible Discovery** as a group (6 minutes). Finally, spend four minutes at the end discussing points that had an impact on participants.

Video Highlights (5 minutes)

> Here you'll ask one or more of the following questions that directly relate to the video the participants have just seen.

1. Look at the map of Israel on page 64 of your Participant's Guide. Note the location of the Via Maris and the valleys that extend from the coastal plain into the Shephelah and the mountains. How does this help you to understand the important role this area played in the lives of the Israelites?

    Suggested Responses: will vary, but the Shephelah was obviously a critical "buffer zone" for people who lived in the mountains or on the coastal plain; it was where the Israelites' culture met the pagan Philistine culture; it was an essential area to control because whoever controlled the Shephelah controlled both the mountains and the coastal plain; with easy access to trade routes, it obviously could have a great impact on world commerce; it was the location of many strategic battles; Israelite control of the Shephelah was crucial to God's plan, etc.

2. What did you learn about the Philistines and their culture that you did not know before watching this video? How does this help you to understand the significance of what took place between the Israelites and the Philistines?

    Suggested Responses: will vary but may include technological superiority, religious ideas and practices, etc.

3. What happened to Samson that caused him to fail to live up to his calling?

    Suggested Responses: He was attracted to the lifestyle and values of the Philistines; he valued the pleasures of life more than his commitment to faithful obedience to God; he did not confront the sin in his own life; he seems to have had much pride in himself; etc.

video Highlights

1. Look at the map of Israel on page 64. Note the location of the Via Maris and the valleys that extend from the coastal plain into the Shephelah and the mountains. How does this help you to understand the important role this area played in the lives of the Israelites?

2. What did you learn about the Philistines and their culture that you did not know before watching this video? How does this help you to understand the significance of what took place between the Israelites and the Philistines?

3. What happened to Samson that caused him to fail to live up to his calling?

4. Eli sent the ark of the covenant into battle, hoping that God would then rescue the Israelites. Why do you think Eli's strategy didn't work? What message does this story have for Christians today?

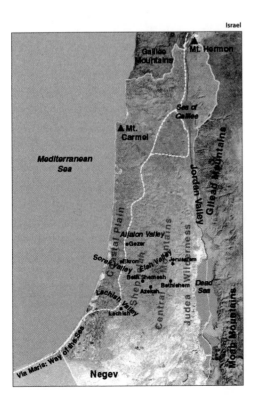

Israel

✏ 4. Eli sent the ark of the covenant into battle, hoping that God would then rescue the Israelites. Why do you think Eli's strategy didn't work? What message does this story have for Christians today?

Suggested Responses: The strategy didn't work because the Israelites had not been faithful in obeying God, and God didn't choose to "bail them out" of their difficulties. This can remind us of the importance of walking with God rather than just calling on Him for help in desperate circumstances.

Israel

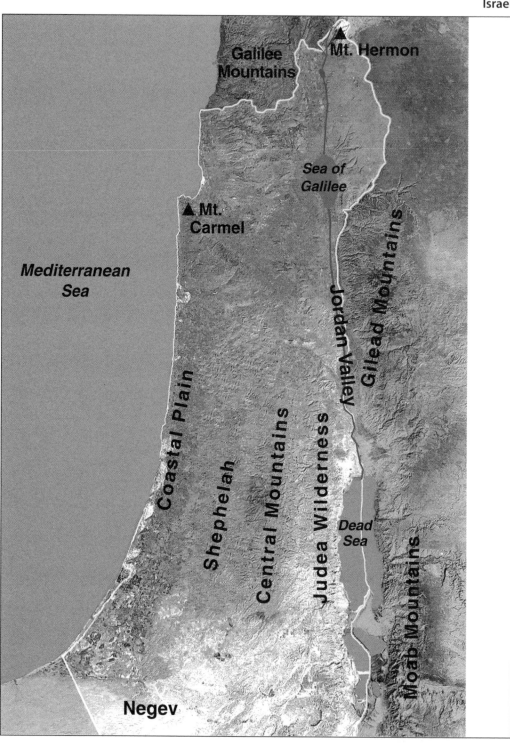

video нighlights

1. Look at the map of Israel on page 64. Note the location of the Via Maris and the valleys that extend from the coastal plain into the Shephelah and the mountains. How does this help you to understand the important role this area played in the lives of the Israelites?

2. What did you learn about the Philistines and their culture that you did not know before watching this video? How does this help you to understand the significance of what took place between the Israelites and the Philistines?

3. What happened to Samson that caused him to fail to live up to his calling?

4. Eli sent the ark of the covenant into battle, hoping that God would then rescue the Israelites. Why do you think Eli's strategy didn't work? What message does this story have for Christians today?

64   Faith Lessons on the Promised Land

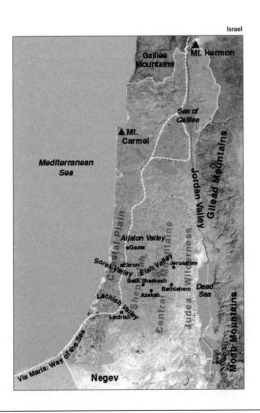

Israel

PLANNING NOTES:

SPOTLIGHT ON THE EVIDENCE

The Making of a Tel

Israel is dotted with distinctive hills called *tels* that are characterized by steep sides and flat tops. (*Tel*, incidentally, is the Hebrew spelling, which we use in this study. The English spelling is *tell*.) These hills comprise layers and layers of ancient settlements, each of which was built on the ruins of a previous settlement. In general terms, here's how tels, including Tel Beth Shemesh, were formed.

Stage 1: People settled on the site, eventually building a wall and gate. Often a rampart was built against the wall to protect the hill from erosion and to keep enemies away from the base of the wall.

Stage 2: The settlement was abandoned, due to war, drought, etc. Then the ruins faded into the landscape.

Stage 3: People moved back to the same spot, filled in holes, gathered larger building stones, leveled off the hill, and rebuilt. Then the city's success attracted enemies . . . and the cycle of destruction and rebuilding continued.

Stage 4: Layers upon layers of ruins accumulated (sort of like a layer cake), so the hill became higher. Each layer—or stratum—records what life was like during a particular time. Artifacts discovered in the tel reveal a great deal about how people lived during specific time periods.

Tels help us understand more clearly the Bible's message by providing relevant information about life in biblical times. Each tel is, in effect, a unique gift from God to help us better understand His Word.

(continued on page 118)

Diagram of a Tel

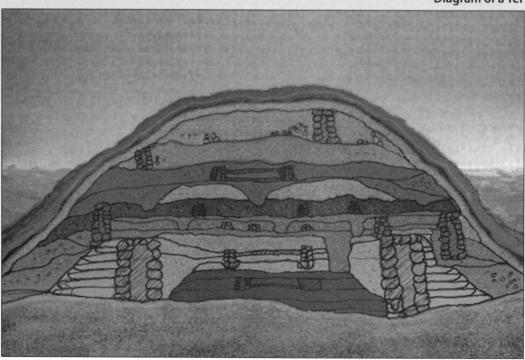

SPOTLIGHT ON THE EVIDENCE

The Making of a Tel

Israel is dotted with distinctive hills called *tels* that are characterized by steep sides and flat tops. (*Tel*, incidentally, is the Hebrew spelling, which we use in this study. The English spelling is *tell*.) These hills comprise layers and layers of ancient settlements, each of which was built on the ruins of a previous settlement. In general terms, here's how tels, including Tel Beth Shemesh, were formed.

Stage 1: People settled on the site, eventually building a wall and gate. Often a rampart was built against the wall to protect the hill from erosion and to keep enemies away from the base of the wall.

Stage 2: The settlement was abandoned, due to war, drought, etc. Then the ruins faded into the landscape.

Stage 3: People moved back to the same spot, filled in holes, gathered larger building stones, leveled off the hill, and rebuilt. Then the city's success attracted enemies . . . and the cycle of destruction and rebuilding continued.

(continued on page 66)

Diagram of a Tel

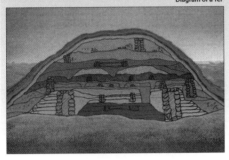

(continued from page 65)

Stage 4: Layers upon layers of ruins accumulated (sort of like a layer cake), so the hill became higher. Each layer—or stratum—records what life was like during a particular time. Artifacts discovered in the tel reveal a great deal about how people lived during specific time periods.

Tels help us understand more clearly the Bible's message by providing relevant information about life in biblical times. Each tel is, in effect, a unique gift from God to help us better understand His Word.

The Making of a City

The environment of the Middle East, including Israel, is harsh and mostly unsuitable for settlement. For a location such as Beth Shemesh to be habitable, three conditions were needed:

Fresh Water

Although rainfall is plentiful in some regions of Israel, most rain falls during the winter. Many ancient communities stored rainwater in cisterns. If a season received below-average rainfall, cisterns dried up and people abandoned their city. If an enemy laid siege to a city, only the cisterns inside the city walls were available, and often the water ran out and the city fell. Jerusalem was built next to the spring of Gihon. Meggido, Hazor, and Gezer had tunnels dug through bedrock in order to reach fresh water.

Profitable Occupation

People needed the opportunity to either grow a consistent food supply or to be able to buy food.

- Olive trees flourished in Judea and Galilee.
- Wheat grew in the valleys of Judea and Jezreel.
- Shepherds raised sheep and goats in the wilderness.
- Chorazin and Ekron had large, olive-oil processing facilities.
- Jerusalem was famous for its purple dye.
- Some cities supplied travelers on the Via Maris, the major trade route.

(continued from page 116)

The Making of a City

The environment of the Middle East, including Israel, is harsh and mostly unsuitable for settlement. For a location such as Beth Shemesh to be habitable, three conditions were needed:

Fresh Water

Although rainfall is plentiful in some regions of Israel, most rain falls during the winter. Many ancient communities stored rainwater in cisterns. If a season received below-average rainfall, cisterns dried up and people abandoned their city. If an enemy laid siege to a city, only the cisterns inside the city walls were available, and often the water ran out and the city fell. Jerusalem was built next to the spring of Gihon. Meggido, Hazor, and Gezer had tunnels dug through bedrock in order to reach fresh water.

Profitable Occupation

People needed the opportunity to either grow a consistent food supply or to be able to buy food.

- Olive trees flourished in Judea and Galilee.
- Wheat grew in the valleys of Judea and Jezreel.
- Shepherds raised sheep and goats in the wilderness.
- Chorazin and Ekron had large, olive-oil processing facilities.
- Jerusalem was famous for its purple dye.
- Some cities supplied travelers on the Via Maris, the major trade route.

A Defensible Location

The political climate in the ancient Middle East was volatile, so cities were typically built on hills ringing fertile valleys so inhabitants could defend themselves.

Why Beth Shemesh?

- Guarded a passage between the coastal plain (Philistine territory) and the mountains of Judah (Israelite territory).
- Was founded during the early Bronze Age—nearly 5,000 years ago.
- Was destroyed and rebuilt at least six times, once by the Babylonians on their way to destroy Jerusalem for the first time (588–587 B.C.).
- Contained many olive oil and fabric dying installations and wheat production industries during King David's time.

(continued from page 65)

Stage 4: Layers upon layers of ruins accumulated (sort of like a layer cake), so the hill became higher. Each layer—or stratum—records what life was like during a particular time. Artifacts discovered in the tel reveal a great deal about how people lived during specific time periods.

Tels help us understand more clearly the Bible's message by providing relevant information about life in biblical times. Each tel is, in effect, a unique gift from God to help us better understand His Word.

The Making of a City

The environment of the Middle East, including Israel, is harsh and mostly unsuitable for settlement. For a location such as Beth Shemesh to be habitable, three conditions were needed:

Fresh Water

Although rainfall is plentiful in some regions of Israel, most rain falls during the winter. Many ancient communities stored rainwater in cisterns. If a season received below-average rainfall, cisterns dried up and people abandoned their city. If an enemy laid siege to a city, only the cisterns inside the city walls were available, and often the water ran out and the city fell. Jerusalem was built next to the spring of Gihon. Meggido, Hazor, and Gezer had tunnels dug through bedrock in order to reach fresh water.

Profitable Occupation

People needed the opportunity to either grow a consistent food supply or to be able to buy food.

- Olive trees flourished in Judea and Galilee.
- Wheat grew in the valleys of Judea and Jezreel.
- Shepherds raised sheep and goats in the wilderness.
- Chorazin and Ekron had large, olive-oil processing facilities.
- Jerusalem was famous for its purple dye.
- Some cities supplied travelers on the Via Maris, the major trade route.

A Defensible Location

The political climate in the ancient Middle East was volatile, so cities were typically built on hills ringing fertile valleys so inhabitants could defend themselves.

Why Beth Shemesh?
- Guarded a passage between the coastal plain (Philistine territory) and the mountains of Judah (Israelite territory).
- Was founded during the early Bronze Age—nearly 5,000 years ago.
- Was destroyed and rebuilt at least six times, once by the Babylonians on their way to destroy Jerusalem for the first time (588–587 B.C.).
- Contained many olive oil and fabric dying installations and wheat production industries during King David's time.

PLANNING NOTES:

Small Group Bible Discovery (6 minutes)

> *Participant's Guide pages 68–73.*
>
> During this time, a group with fewer than seven participants will stay together. A group with seven or more participants will break into small groups and reassemble as a large group during the final four minutes. Assign each group one of the following topics. If you have more than five small groups, assign some topics to more than one group.

Let's break into groups of three to five—people sitting near you—and study some of the Bible passages and truths mentioned in the video.

Turn to pages 68–73 in your Participant's Guide. There you'll find a list of five topics. You'll have six minutes to read and discuss the topic I'll assign to you. Choose one person in your group to be a spokesperson for your group when we discuss these topics later.

> Assign each group a topic.

I'll signal you when one minute is left.

> After five minutes, let participants know that they have one minute remaining. Then reassemble the entire group. After everyone is back together, begin asking one person from each small group to briefly share a key idea with the larger group. In some cases, you may not have time for every group to share their discoveries.

As time allows, let's briefly share the key ideas that your group discussed.

Topic A: The Shephelah

The foothills—the Shephelah—served as a buffer zone between the Philistine territory of the coastal plain and the mountains where the Israelites lived. Because control of the Shephelah ensured the security and power of the dominant culture, many battles between the Philistines and the Israelites took place there. To establish the dominance of His values and to preserve His plan for the salvation of the world, God raised up heroes to confront the Philistines in the Shephelah.

✏ 1. Investigate the following events that took place in the Shephelah. Note where these events took place, who God raised up to battle the Philistines, and the result.

a. 1 Samuel 13:5–7; 14:1–16, 22–23, 31

Suggested Responses: Jonathan (King Saul's son) and his armor bearer went out into the foothills to fight Philistines. God guided them, and the two of them killed about twenty Philistine soldiers. Then God created a panic among the Philistines, who killed one another and ran away. Through this incident and remaining battles that day, God helped His people regain control of the key Shephelah region. (Note: The Aijalon Valley penetrated the

68 Faith Lessons on the Promised Land

small group bible discovery

Topic A: The Shephelah

The foothills—the Shephelah—served as a buffer zone between the Philistine territory of the coastal plain and the mountains where the Israelites lived. Because control of the Shephelah ensured the security and power of the dominant culture, many battles between the Philistines and the Israelites took place there. To establish the dominance of His values and to preserve His plan for the salvation of the world, God raised up heroes to confront the Philistines in the Shephelah.

1. Investigate the following events that took place in the Shephelah. Note where these events took place, who God raised up to battle the Philistines, and the result.

   a. 1 Samuel 13:5–7; 14:1–16, 22–23, 31

   b. 1 Samuel 17:1–9, 16, 32, 48–52

   c. Judges 13:1–5, 24–25; 15:3–5, 14–17

Shephelah between the coastal plain and the mountains. Michmash was at one end of the Aijalon Valley.)

b. 1 Samuel 17:1–9, 16, 32, 48–52

Suggested Responses: The Philistines and Israelites prepared to battle in the foothills (the Elah Valley), and a Philistine champion named Goliath taunted the Israelite soldiers for forty days. After David—a shepherd boy—killed Goliath, the Philistines were routed. They ran to their cities, and many Philistine soldiers were killed as they retreated.

c. Judges 13:1–5, 24–25; 15:3–5, 14–17

Suggested Responses: After God punished Israel for forty years under the Philistines' rule, He gave a son (Samson) to a childless Danite family from Zorah. (Zorah was located in the Sorek Valley.) He was reared as a Nazirite—a man set apart from his culture who would direct people toward God. When he grew older, Samson burned the Philistines' grain, vineyards, and olive groves and killed many Philistines in the Shephelah.

DATA FILE

The Shephelah
- Is a twelve- to fifteen-mile-wide region of foothills in Judea that are located between the coastal plain to the west and the Judea Mountains to the east.
- The valleys of the Shephelah functioned as corridors between the mountains and the coastal plain.
- Served as a place of contact—peaceful or not—where the Israelites interacted with the Philistines. Most Philistine-Israelite conflicts took place here.
- Symbolizes for us the places where God's values meet the pagan practices of Western culture. Like the Israelites, we have a choice: to withdraw to the "mountains" or to be on the front line, confronting the secular values of our world, and with God's blessing seek to gain control of the "coastal plain" in our neighborhoods, cities, country, and the world.

Topic B: The Philistines

1. What do the following passages reveal about the Philistines and their culture?

a. 1 Samuel 13:16–22

Suggested Responses: The Philistines were aggressive, sending out raiding parties of soldiers. Far more advanced than the Israelites, the Philistines knew how to make iron tools and used their superior technology to keep the Israelites in subjection to them.

small Group Bible Discovery

Topic A: The Shephelah

The foothills—the Shephelah—served as a buffer zone between the Philistine territory of the coastal plain and the mountains where the Israelites lived. Because control of the Shephelah ensured the security and power of the dominant culture, many battles between the Philistines and the Israelites took place there. To establish the dominance of His values and to preserve His plan for the salvation of the world, God raised up heroes to confront the Philistines in the Shephelah.

   1. Investigate the following events that took place in the Shephelah. Note where these events took place, who God raised up to battle the Philistines, and the result.

     a. 1 Samuel 13:5–7; 14:1–16, 22–23, 31

     b. 1 Samuel 17:1–9, 16, 32, 48–52

     c. Judges 13:1–5, 24–25; 15:3–5, 14–17

DATA FILE

The Shephelah

- a twelve- to fifteen-mile-wide region of foothills in Judea that are located between the coastal plain to the west and the Judea Mountains to the east.
- The valleys of the Shephelah functioned as corridors between the mountains and the coastal plain.
- Served as a place of contact—peaceful or not—where the Israelites interacted with the Philistines. Most Philistine-Israelite conflicts took place here.
- Symbolizes for us the places where God's values meet the pagan practices of Western culture. Like the Israelites, we have a choice: to withdraw to the "mountains" or to be on the front line, confront the secular values of our world, and with God's blessing seek to gain control of the "coastal plain" in our neighborhoods, cities, country, and the world.

Topic B: The Philistines

   1. What do the following passages reveal about the Philistines and their culture?

     a. 1 Samuel 13:16–22

     b. 1 Samuel 31:1–13

     c. 1 Kings 22:51–53; 2 Kings 1:1–3; Matthew 12:24–28

     d. Judges 1:19; 2:1–3

PLANNING NOTES:

b. 1 Samuel 31:1–13

Suggested Responses: The Philistines were cruel and ruthless enemies. They completely took over the cities and towns of their defeated enemies and stripped dead soldiers of valuables. Saul feared how they would torment him if they captured him alive. The Philistines proclaimed the news of the deaths of King Saul and his three sons in their temple and displayed Saul's armor in the "temple of the Ashtoreths" (the goddess of sexuality whose rituals involved extremely immoral practices). Idol worship was a key part of the Philistines' culture, as evidenced by their use of their temple as a prominent meeting place. They also degraded Saul's dead body, an act that greatly offended the Israelites.

c. 1 Kings 22:51–53; 2 Kings 1:1–3; Matthew 12:24–28

Suggested Responses: Ahaziah, son of Israel's wicked King Ahab, followed in his father's footsteps and worshiped Baal, the god of the Philistines. This demonstrates how much the Philistine culture had influenced the Israelites. (Note: Beelzebub [also known as Baal] was the god of the Philistine city of Ekron. Jesus' identification of Beelzebub with Satan indicates the satanic nature of the Philistines' religion and the pagan values by which they lived. Their rituals involved sacred prostitution and even child sacrifice.)

d. Judges 1:19; 2:1–3

Suggested Responses: The Philistine army was tough to beat because it had iron chariots, which the Israelites didn't have. So the Israelites gave up, in effect giving up their opportunity to influence the culture around them so that the world would know that the Lord was the one true God. Because of the Israelites' lack of faith in God to drive out their enemies before them, God said that the Israelites would be oppressed and ensnared by the cultures of the land.

DATA FILE

The Shephelah

- a twelve- to fifteen-mile-wide region of foothills in Judea that are located between the coastal plain to the west and the Judea Mountains to the east.
- The valleys of the Shephelah functioned as corridors between the mountains and the coastal plain.
- Served as a place of contact—peaceful or not—where the Israelites interacted with the Philistines. Most Philistine-Israelite conflicts took place here.
- Symbolizes for us the places where God's values meet the pagan practices of Western culture. Like the Israelites, we have a choice: to withdraw to the "mountains" or to be on the front line, confront the secular values of our world, and with God's blessing seek to gain control of the "coastal plain" in our neighborhoods, cities, country, and the world.

Topic B: The Philistines

1. What do the following passages reveal about the Philistines and their culture?

    a. 1 Samuel 13:16–22

    b. 1 Samuel 31:1–13

    c. 1 Kings 22:51–53; 2 Kings 1:1–3; Matthew 12:24–28

    d. Judges 1:19; 2:1–3

PLANNING NOTES:

DATA FILE

The Philistines

History

Sailed from the Aegean world (Greece) and settled along the coast of Palestine about 1100 B.C., about the time the Israelites entered the Promised Land from the east. Developed a sophisticated culture in various city states.

Location

The five main Philistine cities were located near the Via Maris trade route, which went through the coastal plain. So, the Philistines dominated world trade and greatly influenced other nations.

Industry

Had an elaborate olive pressing industry. (At Ekron alone, about 200 installations produced olive oil—perhaps more than 1,000 tons!) Also famous for iron making.

Military Might

Philistine soldiers were quite tall, clean shaven, and wore breastplates and small kilts. The soldiers carried small shields and fought with straight swords and spears.

Artistic Skill

Created intricate pottery with red and black geometric designs on white backgrounds.

Religion

Very sophisticated and immoral. The people built carefully planned temples in Gaza, Ashdod, and Beth Shean. Dagon, their main god, was thought to be the god of grain. Believed to be his mistress, the goddess Ashtoreth was associated with war and fertility. Baal-Zebul, thought to be Dagon's son, was worshiped at Ekron.

Topic C: Samson—Set Apart for God

1. Describe the circumstances of Samson's miraculous birth. (See Judges 13:1–14, 24–25.)

    Suggested Responses: The angel of the Lord appeared to the childless wife of Manoah, a Danite. He promised her that she would give birth to a son, then told her that the son would be a Nazirite who would start to deliver Israel from the Philistines' rule. So she told Manoah, who then asked God to send the angel back again to teach them how to rear the boy properly. The angel reappeared and explained things, and later Manoah's wife gave birth to a boy named Samson.

70   Faith Lessons on the Promised Land

DATA FILE

The Philistines

History

Sailed from the Aegean world (Greece) and settled along the coast of Palestine about 1100 B.C., about the time the Israelites entered the Promised Land from the east. Developed a sophisticated culture in various city states.

Location

The five main Philistine cities were located near the Via Maris trade route, which went through the coastal plain. So, the Philistines dominated world trade and greatly influenced other nations.

Industry

Had an elaborate olive pressing industry. (At Ekron alone, about 200 installations produced olive oil—perhaps more than 1,000 tons!) Also famous for iron making.

Military Might

Philistine soldiers were quite tall, clean shaven, and wore breastplates and small kilts. The soldiers carried small shields and fought with straight swords and spears.

Artistic Skill

Created intricate pottery with red and black geometric designs on white backgrounds.

Religion

Very sophisticated and immoral. The people built carefully planned temples in Gaza, Ashdod, and Beth Shean. Dagon, their main god, was thought to be the god of grain. Believed to be his mistress, the goddess Ashtoreth was associated with war and fertility. Baal-Zebul, thought to be Dagon's son, was worshiped at Ekron.

Session Four: Confronting Evil   71

Topic C: Samson—Set Apart for God

1. Describe the circumstances of Samson's miraculous birth. (See Judges 13:1–14, 24–25.)

2. Describe what each of the following passages says about what it means to be a Nazirite:

   a. Numbers 6:1–3

   b. Numbers 6:4

   c. Numbers 6:5

   d. Numbers 6:6–7

   e. Numbers 6:8

   f. Numbers 6:9–12

✏ 2. Describe what each of the following passages says about what it means to be a Nazirite:

a. Numbers 6:1–3

Suggested Responses: The person makes a special vow of separation to the Lord: must not drink grape juice, vinegar, wine, or other fermented drink; must not eat raisins or grapes. (Note: fresh water was hard to come by.)

b. Numbers 6:4

Suggested Responses: The Nazirite must not eat anything from a grapevine. (Note: Some scholars believe that the grape symbolized the fertility of Canaan in the same way wheat represents the abundance of the state of Kansas. So the person who avoided grapes in any form displayed a willingness to reject the Canaanites' belief in the gods of fertility who supposedly caused the grapes to grow.)

c. Numbers 6:5

Suggested Responses: As long as he is a Nazirite, he must not cut his hair. (Note: The appearance of an unshaven separatist would have created quite a stir in society.)

d. Numbers 6:6–7

Suggested Response: A Nazirite is not to go near a dead body, even the body of a close family member.

e. Numbers 6:8

Suggested Response: A Nazirite is to remain consecrated to God during the entire period of his vow of separation.

f. Numbers 6:9–12

Suggested Responses: If someone dies in his presence, thus defiling his hair, the Nazirite must shave his head on the seventh day of cleansing and bring two doves or young pigeons on the eighth day to the priest, who would make the required offerings.

Topic C: Samson—Set Apart for God

1. Describe the circumstances of Samson's miraculous birth. (See Judges 13:1–14, 24–25.)

2. Describe what each of the following passages says about what it means to be a Nazirite:

   a. Numbers 6:1–3

   b. Numbers 6:4

   c. Numbers 6:5

   d. Numbers 6:6–7

   e. Numbers 6:8

   f. Numbers 6:9–12

PLANNING NOTES:

Topic D: Samson and the Philistines—Confrontation and Compromise

✏ 1. Samson sought opportunities to confront the Philistines. What was his intent in each of the following encounters?

Judges 14:1–4	He sought a Philistine wife in order to confront the Philistines.
Judges 15:1–5	After Samson's father-in-law gave his wife to another man, Samson caught 300 foxes, tied them tail to tail in pairs, attached torches to their tails, and set the foxes loose in the Philistines' standing grain. The resulting fires burned up all the grain, vineyards, and olive groves.
Judges 15:9–15	Angered by the fire damage Samson had caused, the Philistines prepared for war. Afraid, men from Judah went to capture Samson and hand him over to the Philistines. Samson allowed the Israelite men to tie him with new ropes, but as they approached the Philistines, God's power came upon Samson. He broke loose and killed a thousand Philistine men with the jawbone of a donkey.

✏ 2. In what ways did Samson violate his Nazirite vow and compromise his calling?

a. Numbers 6:6–7; Judges 14:5–9

Suggested Responses: Samson touched and later ate from the body of a dead lion.

b. Numbers 6:4; Judges 14:10

Suggested Responses: Samson threw a feast during his wedding celebration. (Note: the word translated "feast" means "drinking bout" or "orgy of drinking.") Thus he drank wine.

c. Judges 16:1–3

Suggested Responses: Samson went to the Philistine city of Gaza and spent part of the night with a prostitute.

Topic E: God Uses Failure to Accomplish His Purposes

✏ 1. What were the short-term and long-term consequences of Samson's relationship with Delilah, a Philistine woman living in the Sorek Valley?

Short-term Consequences	Long-term Consequences
Judges 16:5, 16–21	Judges 16:23–30
Delilah finally extracted the secret of Samson's strength. The Philistines captured him, blinded him, and forced him to grind grain in the prison.	The Philistines summoned Samson from prison for their amusement during their celebration and sacrifice to Dagon. His hair had once again grown, and he prayed for God to strengthen him so that he could pull the house (temple) down. God answered, and Samson killed more Philistines by his death than he had killed during his life.

Topic D: Samson and the Philistines—Confrontation and Compromise

1. Samson sought opportunities to confront the Philistines. What was his intent in each of the following encounters?

Judges 14:1–4	
Judges 15:1–5	
Judges 15:9–15	

2. In what ways did Samson violate his Nazirite vow and compromise his calling?

   a. Numbers 6:6–7; Judges 14:5–9

   b. Numbers 6:4; Judges 14:10

   c. Judges 16:1–3

Topic E: God Uses Failure to Accomplish His Purposes

1. What were the short-term and long-term consequences of Samson's relationship with Delilah, a Philistine woman living in the Sorek Valley?

Short-term Consequences	Long-term Consequences
Judges 16:5, 16–21	Judges 16:23–30

2. Clearly God can use human failure and weakness to accomplish His purposes. Describe the weaknesses of the following people and how God used them.

   a. Moses (See Exodus 3:9–11; 4:1, 10–16; 33:12–17.)

   b. David (See 2 Samuel 11:1–5, 14–17; 12:24.)

   c. Peter (See Luke 22:54–62; John 21:15–19.)

✏ 2.   Clearly God can use human failure and weakness to accomplish His purposes. Describe the weaknesses of the following people and how God used them.

   a.   Moses (See Exodus 3:9–11; 4:1, 10–16; 33:12–17.)

        Suggested Responses: Moses didn't believe he could be God's chosen leader, yet he led the Israelites out of Egypt and pleased the Lord.

   b.   David (See 2 Samuel 11:1–5, 14–17; 12:24.)

        Suggested Responses: David committed adultery with Bathsheba and had her husband murdered, yet out of the union with Bathsheba came Solomon, a great king of Israel.

   c.   Peter (See Luke 22:54–62; John 21:15–19.)

        Suggested Responses: Although Peter denied Jesus three times, God forgave him and allowed him to become a pillar of the early church.

faith Lesson

6 minutes   **Time for Reflection (4 minutes)**

It's time for each of us to think quietly about how we can apply what we've learned today. On pages 74–75 of your Participant's Guide, you'll find a passage of Scripture. Let's each read this passage silently and take the next few minutes to consider some of the questions that follow the Scripture passage.

Please do not talk during this time. It's a time when we all can reflect on the ways in which God would have us confront the culture of our world.

> *The Scripture passage and questions are reproduced in their entirety in the Participant's Guide on pages 74–75.*

   Some time later, he [Samson] fell in love with a woman in the Valley of Sorek whose name was Delilah. The rulers of the Philistines went to her and said, "See if you can lure him into showing you the secret of his great strength and how we can overpower him so we may tie him up and subdue him. Each one of us will give you eleven hundred shekels of silver." . . .

   Having put him to sleep on her lap, she called a man to shave off the seven braids of his hair, and so began to subdue him. And his strength left him.

   Then she called, "Samson, the Philistines are upon you!"

   He awoke from his sleep and thought, "I'll go out as before and shake myself free." But he did not know that the LORD had left him.

   Then the Philistines seized him, gouged out his eyes and took him down to Gaza. Binding him with bronze shackles, they set him to grinding in the prison. . . .

Topic E: God Uses Failure to Accomplish His Purposes

1. What were the short-term and long-term consequences of Samson's relationship with Delilah, a Philistine woman living in the Sorek Valley?

Short-term Consequences	Long-term Consequences
Judges 16:5, 16–21	Judges 16:23–30

2. Clearly God can use human failure and weakness to accomplish His purposes. Describe the weaknesses of the following people and how God used them.

   a. Moses (See Exodus 3:9–11; 4:1, 10–16; 33:12–17.)

   b. David (See 2 Samuel 11:1–5, 14–17; 12:24.)

   c. Peter (See Luke 22:54–62; John 21:15–19.)

faith Lesson

Time for Reflection

Please read the following passage of Scripture silently and take the next few minutes to reflect on the ways in which God would have you confront the culture of your world.

Some time later, he [Samson] fell in love with a woman in the Valley of Sorek whose name was Delilah. The rulers of the Philistines went to her and said, "See if you can lure him into showing you the secret of his great strength and how we can overpower him so we may tie him up and subdue him. Each one of us will give you eleven hundred shekels of silver." . . .

Having put him to sleep on her lap, she called a man to shave off the seven braids of his hair, and so began to subdue him. And his strength left him.

Then she called, "Samson, the Philistines are upon you!"

He awoke from his sleep and thought, "I'll go out as before and shake myself free." But he did not know that the Lord had left him.

Then the Philistines seized him, gouged out his eyes and took him down to Gaza. Binding him with bronze shackles, they set him to grinding in the prison. . . .

Now the rulers of the Philistines assembled to offer a great sacrifice to Dagon their god and to celebrate, saying, "Our god has delivered Samson, our enemy, into our hands."

When the people saw him, they praised their god, saying, "Our god has delivered our enemy into our hands, the one who laid waste our land and multiplied our slain."

While they were in high spirits, they shouted, "Bring out Samson to entertain us." So they called Samson out of the prison, and he performed for them.

When they stood him among the pillars, Samson said to the servant who held his hand, "Put me where I can feel the pillars that support the temple, so that I may lean against them." Now the temple

Now the rulers of the Philistines assembled to offer a great sacrifice to Dagon their god and to celebrate, saying, "Our god has delivered Samson, our enemy, into our hands."

When the people saw him, they praised their god, saying, "Our god has delivered our enemy into our hands, the one who laid waste our land and multiplied our slain."

While they were in high spirits, they shouted, "Bring out Samson to entertain us." So they called Samson out of the prison, and he performed for them.

When they stood him among the pillars, Samson said to the servant who held his hand, "Put me where I can feel the pillars that support the temple, so that I may lean against them." Now the temple was crowded with men and women; all the rulers of the Philistines were there, and on the roof were about three thousand men and women watching Samson perform. Then Samson prayed to the LORD, "O Sovereign LORD, remember me. O God, please strengthen me just once more, and let me with one blow get revenge on the Philistines for my two eyes." Then Samson reached toward the two central pillars on which the temple stood. Bracing himself against them, his right hand on the one and his left hand on the other, Samson said, "Let me die with the Philistines!" Then he pushed with all his might, and down came the temple on the rulers and all the people in it. Thus he killed many more when he died than while he lived.

JUDGES 16:4–5, 19–21, 23–30

1. In light of Samson's lusty willfulness, what change in attitude is evident in his final prayer to God? What was the result of his prayer?

2. Samson clearly had many faults, yet God used him to challenge the Philistines' power. Consider a time in your life when God used your weakness, or that of other people, as an opportunity to demonstrate His strength. What difference can God make in your life now, even when you feel inadequate to face a difficult challenge?

3. Which sinful aspect(s) of modern culture is attractive to you? Wealth? Pleasure? Gratification? Recognition? What might you do to stand firm when you are tempted to compromise God's values?

4. God gave Samson a mission—to overcome the power of evil that was threatening His people. In what way(s) is the mission God has given you similar to that of Samson?

As soon as participants have spent four minutes reflecting on the above questions, get the entire group's attention and move to the next section.

was crowded with men and women; all the rulers of the Philistines were there, and on the roof were about three thousand men and women watching Samson perform. Then Samson prayed to the LORD, "O Sovereign LORD, remember me. O God, please strengthen me just once more, and let me with one blow get revenge on the Philistines for my two eyes." Then Samson reached toward the two central pillars on which the temple stood. Bracing himself against them, his right hand on the one and his left hand on the other, Samson said, "Let me die with the Philistines!" Then he pushed with all his might, and down came the temple on the rulers and all the people in it. Thus he killed many more when he died than while he lived.

JUDGES 16:4–5, 19–21, 23–30

1. In light of Samson's lusty willfulness, what change in attitude is evident in his final prayer to God? What was the result of his prayer?

2. Samson clearly had many faults, yet God used him to challenge the Philistines' power. Consider a time in your life when God used your weakness, or that of other people, as an opportunity to demonstrate His strength. What difference can God make in your life now, even when you feel inadequate to face a difficult challenge?

3. Which sinful aspects of modern culture are attractive to you? Wealth? Pleasure? Gratification? Recognition? What might you do to stand firm when you are tempted to compromise God's values?

4. God gave Samson a mission—to overcome the power of evil that was threatening His people. In what way(s) is the mission God has given you similar to that of Samson?

Action Points

The key points of this session are outlined below. Consider each point and jot down an action step (or steps) that you will commit to this week as a result of what you have learned today.

1. *As God's people, we—like Samson and the tribe of Dan— are called to be part of the confrontation between God and the ungodliness of the world.* Our calling is to live on the front lines—in our equivalent of the Shephelah, the place where opposing values clash—in order to confront secular values and influence the world for God. But we can only live out a God-centered lifestyle if we refuse to adopt the ungodly values of our culture. Thus we are to remain distinct from the world's culture, not to compromise with it.

PLANNING NOTES:

Action Points (2 minutes)

> *The following points are reproduced on pages 76–78 of the Participant's Guide:*

Now it's time to wrap up our session.

> Give participants a moment to transition from their thoughtfulness to giving you their full attention.

I'd like to take a moment to summarize the key points we explored. After I have reviewed each point, I will give you a moment to jot down an action step (or steps) that you will commit to this week as a result of what you have learned today.

> Read the following points and pause after each so that participants can consider and write out their commitment.

1. *As God's people, we—like Samson and the tribe of Dan—are called to be part of the confrontation between God and the ungodliness of the world.* Our calling is to live on the front lines—in our equivalent of the Shephelah, the place where opposing values clash—in order to confront secular values and influence the world for God. But we can only live out a God-centered lifestyle if we refuse to adopt the ungodly values of our culture. Thus we are to remain distinct from the world's culture, not to compromise with it.

   Which aspects of your culture do you believe God would have you confront?

   In what ways might you be trying to avoid the battles instead of "living in the Shephelah"—the place where God's values meet the pagan practices of your culture?

   In what ways have you compromised with ungodly values around you and weakened the impact God wants you to make instead of being "set apart" for Him and His purposes?

2. *When God calls us to accomplish a specific task, it is essential that we complete it fully.* If we don't, then we—like the tribe of Dan that failed to chase the Philistines out of the land God had provided for His people—jeopardize the whole mission. But when we place all aspects of our lives under the dominion of God's value system and live in close relationship with Him, God will work through us! We can have a powerful impact. We can be like standing stones that represent God and His power to our culture.

   What areas of your life have you not completely and distinctively committed to God and His way of life? What are you going to do about it?

   If you were to apply the same kind of dedication to your personal mission as the Nazirites did during ancient times, how would your life be different?

3. Which sinful aspects of modern culture are attractive to you? Wealth? Pleasure? Gratification? Recognition? What might you do to stand firm when you are tempted to compromise God's values?

4. God gave Samson a mission—to overcome the power of evil that was threatening His people. In what way(s) is the mission God has given you similar to that of Samson?

Action Points

The key points of this session are outlined below. Consider each point and jot down an action step (or steps) that you will commit to this week as a result of what you have learned today.

1. *As God's people, we—like Samson and the tribe of Dan—are called to be part of the confrontation between God and the ungodliness of the world.* Our calling is to live on the front lines—in our equivalent of the Shephelah, the place where opposing values clash—in order to confront secular values and influence the world for God. But we can only live out a God-centered lifestyle if we refuse to adopt the ungodly values of our culture. Thus we are to remain distinct from the world's culture, not to compromise with it.

Which aspects of your culture do you believe God would have you confront?

In what ways might you be trying to avoid the battles instead of "living in the Shephelah"—the place where God's values meet the pagan practices of your culture?

In what ways have you compromised with ungodly values around you and weakened the impact God wants you to make instead of being "set apart" for Him and His purposes?

2. *When God calls us to accomplish a specific task, it is essential that we complete it fully.* If we don't, then we—like the tribe of Dan that failed to chase the Philistines out of the land God had provided for His people—jeopardize the whole mission. But when we place all aspects of our lives under the dominion of God's value system and live in close relationship with Him, God will work through us! We can have a powerful impact. We can be like standing stones that represent God and His power to our culture.

PLANNING NOTES:

closing prayer

I minute

I hope that this lesson has challenged you, as it has me, to think about ways in which we can, in the strength of God's power, confront evil around us. Let's close in prayer.

Dear God, thank You for placing us in unique positions in our culture where we can be godly influences. Please give us the wisdom to recognize the Philistines in our own culture and the courage to live in today's Shephelah—at the cutting edge of culture. Give us courage to confront ungodly, evil values. Help us to remain devoted to You and not get sidetracked by anything that will draw us away from You. Only You can give us the strength to confront evil, to make a difference, to point other people toward You. Thank You for being with us. In Your name we pray, Jesus. Amen.

PLANNING NOTES:

Iron of culture

Before You Lead

Synopsis

This video was filmed at Tel Azekah, a five-acre site that overlooks the Valley of Elah where David killed Goliath. Today Tel Azekah stands as a reminder that the defense of the Shephelah—the foothills between the coastal plains where the Philistines lived and the mountains where the Israelites lived—was critical to the Israelites' survival. To the east of Azekah are the Judea Mountains. To the west, within sight, is the Mediterranean Sea.

Azekah guarded an important gateway into the mountains. The Valley of Elah provided access to Bethlehem, which was a mere twelve miles away from Azekah, and to Jerusalem, which was a few miles north of Bethlehem. For that reason, the Philistines and other pagan cultures wanted to capture and hold Azekah. Even the great empires of the east, Babylon and Assyria, came down the coastal plain and used the Valley of Elah to enter the Shephelah. The Assyrian army of King Sennacherib destroyed Azekah. So did King Nebuchadnezzar of Babylon, who destroyed Azekah in 587 B.C. on his way to destroy the temple in Jerusalem.

This session focuses on the battle between the Philistines and the Israelites that took place in the Valley of Elah during the reign of King Saul. Imagine the scene. Both armies faced one another. A hardened Philistine warrior more than nine feet tall named Goliath taunted the Israelite army every day for forty days and ridiculed their God. Then a young shepherd boy named David, who was perhaps ten or twelve years old, came from Bethlehem in the Judea Mountains to bring food to his brothers, who were Israelite soldiers. This young boy, appalled by the insults the giant hurled at the God of Israel, was compelled by the Spirit of God to fight him.

David had no sword or spear. He couldn't even wear King Saul's armor as protection. He carried a simple sling into battle. Humanly speaking, the boy had little to offer. But he did have a powerful faith in the God of Israel.

Goliath, the Philistine warrior, was equipped with the latest weapons. He carried a sword, a javelin, and an iron-tipped spear. He wore a suit of armor that weighed 125 pounds. His people were masters at making and using iron. It is likely that the Philistines introduced iron making to the Middle East. Because of their ability to work iron, the Philistines had become the predominant culture. They dominated not only in warfare but in material prosperity, commerce, and other areas of technology.

The Israelites, on the other hand, didn't know how to work with iron and even had to go to the Philistines to have their tools sharpened (1 Samuel 13:19–21). On the day of battle, only two Israelite soldiers—King Saul and his son,

Jonathan—possessed a sword or spear (1 Samuel 13:22). No wonder the Israelites were afraid!

Goliath represented more than a formidable military challenge. He represented evil. His armor is described as having "scales"—like the snake Satan embodied while tempting Adam and Eve. David recognized the true nature of Goliath's challenge and accepted it with the correct underlying motive—so that the world would "know that there is a God in Israel." Shortly afterward, David's stone knocked Goliath to the ground, and David drew Goliath's sword and cut off the giant's head.

After that and other victories, King Saul became jealous of David and tried to kill him. David, his men, and their families then fled to Achish, the Philistine king of Gath (1 Samuel 27), who gave David the Philistine city of Ziklag. About the time David became king of Israel years later, the Israelites had learned to work iron and became the dominant culture in the region (2 Samuel 5:17–25). Consequently, the Philistines lost power and influence. It is possible that David (or one of his men) uncovered the Philistine's secret of iron technology while living in Gath and brought it to the Israelites.

Key Points of This Lesson

1. *God can use people who seem to have little to offer to accomplish His purposes.* When we seek to accomplish God's work, our motivation and faith in God is far more significant than our talent or resources. David, for example, was a young shepherd who appeared to have little to offer, but he acted as God's representative. He used his training and primitive tools in order to reveal the God of Israel to the world of his day. He used a simple sling to throw a stone at a man who had the best military technology an advanced culture could offer—and he triumphed because God honored his throw.

2. *God wants each of us to use our particular gifts and talents to influence our culture for Him.* David did what God had qualified and gifted him to do, and because David was motivated by righteousness, he made a powerful impact on his culture. Likewise, we don't have to be anything other than the people God has created us to be in order to accomplish His purposes. Who He has made us to be is good enough. We need only to express the gifts and talents He has given us.

3. *God wants us to use every resource, including the tools and technology of our culture—its "iron"—to accomplish His purposes.* The Israelites achieved a decisive victory over the Philistines when David killed Goliath. Unfortunately, the Philistines remained the superior culture for quite a while afterward (1 Samuel 31). Only when the Israelites, under the reign of faithful King David, harnessed the Philistines' advanced iron technology and used it for God's purposes did they become a great influence and power. Today, Christians who hold a Bible-based value system and are able to shape and control the "iron" of their society will greatly impact their culture.

Session Outline (53 minutes)

I. **Introduction** (4 minutes)

Welcome

What's to Come

Questions to Think About

II. **Show Video "Iron of Culture"** (20 minutes)

III. **Group Discovery** (20 minutes)

Video Highlights

Small Group Bible Discovery

IV. **Faith Lesson** (8 minutes)

Time for Reflection

Action Points

V. **Closing Prayer** (1 minute)

Materials

No additional materials are needed for this session. Simply view the video prior to leading the session so you are familiar with its main points.

PLANNING NOTES:

Iron of Culture

Introduction

Welcome

> Assemble the participants together. Welcome them to session five of *Faith Lessons on the Promised Land.*

What's to Come

In this lesson, we'll gain new insights into the well-known story of David and Goliath. We'll learn how the Philistines had become so powerful and why the Israelites were so afraid of them. We'll see why the cities of the Shephelah were so important to Israel's survival. Also, using David as an illustration, Ray Vander Laan will help us to understand that simply by using our God-given gifts and abilities we can have a powerful influence for God in our culture.

Questions to Think About

> *Participant's Guide page 79.*

> Ask each question and solicit a few responses from group members.

1. Think about a time when you were matched against a formidable opponent. Perhaps when you wanted a particular job but were not as qualified as other applicants. Perhaps when you were bidding for a contract but your company was not as large or well known as your competitors. Perhaps when you were treated unfairly and sought justice. Perhaps when your team had a 2–7 record and you faced a team with a 9–0 record. How did you feel in that situation?

   Suggested Responses: These will vary, but may include feeling lonely, afraid, insignificant, vulnerable, uneasy, discouraged, foolish, etc.

144

SESSION FIVE

iron of culture

questions to think about

1. Think about a time when you were matched against a formidable opponent. Perhaps when you wanted a particular job but were not as qualified as other applicants. Perhaps when you were bidding for a contract but your company was not as large or well known as your competitors. Perhaps when you were treated unfairly and sought justice. Perhaps when your team had a 2–7 record and you faced a team with a 9–0 record. How did you feel in that situation?

2. When you find yourself in a difficult situation in which you feel insecure, how do you tend to respond?

79

PLANNING NOTES:

✏ 2. When you find yourself in a difficult situation in which you feel insecure, how do you tend to respond?

Suggested Responses: These will vary, but may include trying to pretend to be secure, escaping the situation altogether, finding someone to help me get through the situation, admitting my fears to myself and God, turning to God for help, giving up, trying even harder, etc.

Let's keep these feelings in mind as we view the video.

video presentation

20 minutes

| Participant's Guide page 80. |

On page 80 of your Participant's Guide, you will find a space in which to take notes on key points as we watch this video.

Leader's Video Observations

Azekah

Goliath

David

Using Our Gifts to Shape the "Iron" of Society

SESSION FIVE

Iron of Culture

Questions to Think About

1. Think about a time when you were matched against a formidable opponent. Perhaps when you wanted a particular job but were not as qualified as other applicants. Perhaps when you were bidding for a contract but your company was not as large or well known as your competitors. Perhaps when you were treated unfairly and sought justice. Perhaps when your team had a 2–7 record and you faced a team with a 9–0 record. How did you feel in that situation?

2. When you find yourself in a difficult situation in which you feel insecure, how do you tend to respond?

79

80   Faith Lessons on the Promised Land

Video Notes

Azekah

Goliath

David

Using Our Gifts to Shape the "Iron" of Society

Group Discovery

20 minutes

> If your group has seven or more members, use the **Video Highlights** with the entire group (5 minutes), then break into small groups of three to five to discuss the **Small Group Bible Discovery** (10 minutes). Then reassemble the group to discuss the key points discovered (5 minutes).
>
> If your group has fewer than seven members, begin with the **Video Highlights** (5 minutes), then do one or more of the topics found in the **Small Group Bible Discovery** as a group (10 minutes). Finally, spend five minutes at the end discussing points that had an impact on participants.

Video Highlights (5 minutes)

> Here you'll ask one or more of the following questions that directly relate to the video the participants have just seen.

Note the map of Israel on page 82 of your Participant's Guide and locate Azekah and Socoh. Note how far into the Shephelah Azekah is.

1. Why was what happened between David and Goliath in the Elah Valley so critical to the Israelites' survival?

   Suggested Responses: It was critical that the Israelites—who had God on their side—stand up to the powerful Philistines, who had iron weaponry; that the Israelites hold Azekah in order to protect their mountain territory; that they be reminded of their covenant with God—His role in their lives, their need to obey and rely on Him; etc.

2. Goliath said to David, "Am I a dog that you come at me with sticks?" What did the video reveal about why David had primitive weapons?

   Suggested Response: The Israelites had nothing but primitive weapons because they didn't yet know how to work iron. Goliath, on the other hand, probably had his pick of sophisticated weapons, including shields, swords, and spears.

3. If you had been an Israelite soldier, how might you have felt when you faced the weaponry of the Philistines—and the taunts of Goliath?

   Suggested Responses: fearful, wondering how God would work things out, unwilling to go against that proven giant, humiliated that I didn't have the courage to challenge Goliath, ashamed, angry that he would say those things against God, etc.

4. What finally enabled the Israelites to become a significant and influential power in their culture?

   Suggested Response: They once again turned to God, and they obtained the iron-related technology that gave them power in their world and used that technology for God.

video highlights

Note the map of Israel on page 82 and locate Azekah and Socoh. Note how far into the Shephelah Azekah is.

1. Why was what happened between David and Goliath in the Elah Valley so critical to the Israelites' survival?

2. Goliath said to David, "Am I a dog that you come at me with sticks?" What did the video reveal about why David had primitive weapons?

3. If you had been an Israelite soldier, how might you have felt when you faced the weaponry of the Philistines—and the taunts of Goliath?

4. What finally enabled the Israelites to become a significant and influential power in their culture?

PLANNING NOTES:

Israel

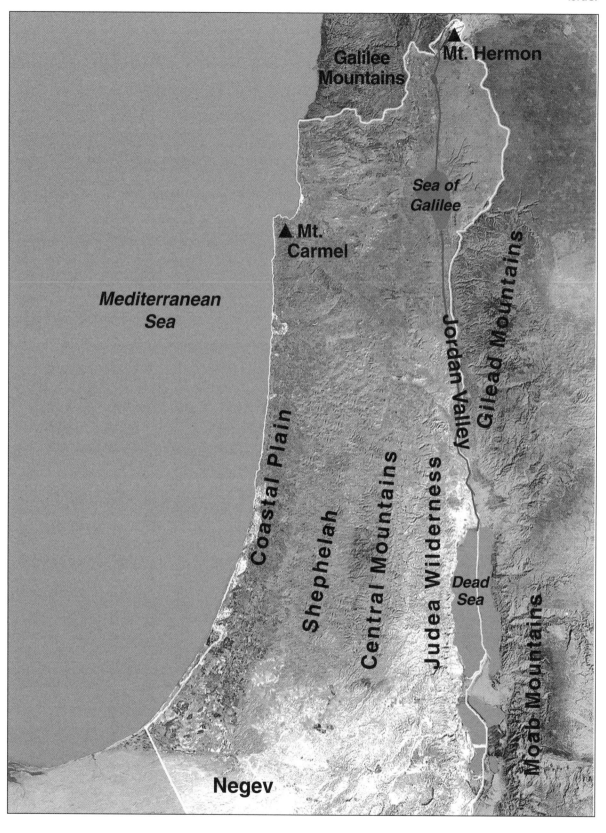

82   Faith Lessons on the Promised Land

DATA FILE

Metalworking in the Middle East

Before 1200 B.C., bronze—a combination of copper and tin—was *the* metal used in the Middle East. Perhaps this was because the melting point of copper is 1,100 degrees Celsius and the melting point of iron is 1,550 degrees Celsius. Although bronze was a significant step beyond stone and wood, it was soft and didn't hold an edge well.

As the Bronze Age ended, many changes occurred. There were many invasions (both the Philistines and Israelites entered Canaan at this time), wars, and collapses of cultures. This resulted in a worldwide shortage of tin, which led to a scarcity of bronze.

During the thirteenth century B.C., an Aegean people—the Philistines—migrated to the Middle East. They may not have invented iron technology, but they used it effectively. In fact, they developed a process that included leaving iron in the fire long enough to absorb the carbon from firewood to form another more malleable form of iron—steel. This superior metal so revolutionized the world that it gave its name to the next 600 years—the Iron Age.

Iron, as a technological advancement during biblical times, could be compared to nuclear energy or computers today. It determined which cultures would dominate world events. It revolutionized how people lived—how much land they could plow, how much stone they could shape, how much wood they could cut. And it changed warfare greatly, just as gunpowder did centuries later.

The pagan Philistine culture dominated the Middle East during the early Iron Age, much as Western nations shape the cultures of developing nations today. The Philistines kept their iron technology secret so others could not use it. Since they lived on the coastal plain along the international trade route, they could also influence the world (a mission God had intended the Israelites to fulfill). The Israelites, on the other hand, did not even own swords and spears—and had to pay the Philistines to sharpen their tools (1 Samuel 13:19–22).

Between the time David killed Goliath and when he became king of Israel (2 Samuel 5), the Israelites learned the secret of iron technology and became the dominant culture (until they were unfaithful to God). Some scholars believe that David, or one of his people, learned this secret while living with the Philistines (1 Samuel 27–29). Although iron technology enabled David to destroy the enemies of God's people, he could not have been as successful as he was without God's hand upon him. Iron technology was one of the means by which God blessed David and provided a people, nation, and kingly pattern for the coming Son of David.

DATA FILE

Metalworking in the Middle East

Before 1200 B.C., bronze—a combination of copper and tin—was *the* metal used in the Middle East. Perhaps this was because the melting point of copper is 1,100 degrees Celsius and the melting point of iron is 1,550 degrees Celsius. Although bronze was a significant step beyond stone and wood, it was soft and didn't hold an edge well.

As the Bronze Age ended, many changes occurred. There were many invasions (both the Philistines and Israelites entered Canaan at this time), wars, and collapses of cultures. This resulted in a worldwide shortage of tin, which led to a scarcity of bronze.

During the thirteenth century B.C., an Aegean people—the Philistines—migrated to the Middle East. They may not have invented iron technology, but they used it effectively. In fact, they developed a process that included leaving iron in the fire long enough to absorb the carbon from firewood to form another more malleable form of iron—steel. This superior metal so revolutionized the world that it gave its name to the next 600 years—the Iron Age.

Iron, as a technological advancement during biblical times, could be compared to nuclear energy or computers today. It determined which cultures would dominate world events. It revolutionized how people lived—how much land they could plow, how much stone they could shape, how much wood they could cut. And it changed warfare greatly, just as gunpowder did centuries later.

The pagan Philistine culture dominated the Middle East during the early Iron Age, much as Western nations shape the cultures of developing nations today. The Philistines kept their iron technology secret so others could not use it. Since they lived on the coastal plain along the international trade route, they could also influence the world (a mission God had intended the Israelites to fulfill). The Israelites, on the other hand, did not even own swords and spears—and had to pay the Philistines to sharpen their tools (1 Samuel 13:19–22).

(continued on page 84)

(continued from page 83)

Between the time David killed Goliath and when he became king of Israel (2 Samuel 5), the Israelites learned the secret of iron technology and became the dominant culture (until they were unfaithful to God). Some scholars believe that David, or one of his people, learned this secret while living with the Philistines (1 Samuel 27–29). Although iron technology enabled David to destroy the enemies of God's people, he could not have been as successful as he was without God's hand upon him. Iron technology was one of the means by which God blessed David and provided a people, nation, and kingly pattern for the coming Son of David.

PLANNING NOTES:

Small Group Bible Discovery (10 minutes)

> *Participant's Guide pages 85–92.*
>
> During this time, a group with fewer than seven participants will stay together. A group with seven or more participants will break into small groups and reassemble as a large group during the final five minutes. Assign each group one of the following topics. If you have more than five small groups, assign some topics to more than one group.

Let's break into groups of three to five—people sitting near you—and study some of the Bible passages and truths mentioned in the video.

Turn to pages 85–92 in your Participant's Guide. There you'll find five topics. You'll have ten minutes to read and discuss the topic I'll assign to you. Choose one person in your group to be a spokesperson for your group when we discuss these topics later.

> Assign each group a topic.

I'll signal you when one minute is left.

> After nine minutes, let participants know that they have one minute remaining. Then reassemble the entire group. After everyone is back together, begin asking one person from each small group to briefly share a key idea with the larger group. In some cases, you may not have time for every group to share their discoveries.

As time allows, let's briefly share the key ideas that your group discussed.

Topic A: A Clash of Cultures

The battle in the Elah Valley is significant not because David, a young shepherd who was untrained in warfare, defeated Goliath, a giant of a warrior, but because of what the battle represented.

1. Read 1 Samuel 17:1–3 and answer the following questions.

   a. Describe how the two armies positioned themselves for battle in the Shephelah region.

   Suggested Responses: The Philistine soldiers came up into the Shephelah from the coastal plain and camped between Socoh and Azekah. They positioned themselves on one hill overlooking the Elah Valley. The Israelite soldiers assembled and camped in the Valley of Elah and gathered on a hill on the other side of the valley.

   b. Which army was the aggressor?

   Suggested Response: The Philistine army, which came from the coastal plain into the Shephelah.

small group bible discovery

Topic A: A Clash of Cultures

The battle in the Elah Valley is significant not because David, a young shepherd who was untrained in warfare, defeated Goliath, a giant of a warrior, but because of what the battle represented.

1. Read 1 Samuel 17:1–3 and answer the following questions.

   a. Describe how the two armies positioned themselves for battle in the Shephelah region.

   b. Which army was the aggressor?

   c. Why was this an important battle for both sides?

2. Read 1 Samuel 17:4–7, 51 and describe the kind of warrior Goliath was.

PLANNING NOTES:

c. Why was this an important battle for both sides?

Suggested Responses: Whoever won the battle would gain control of the Shephelah and thereby dominate the region; the victor would be able to influence other people who passed through the area; it was a battle of culture and values; ultimately it was a battle between God and Satan.

✏ 2. Read 1 Samuel 17:4–7, 51 and describe the kind of warrior Goliath was.

Suggested Responses: He was a skilled, trained warrior—a champion—who had defeated his enemies time and again. He was six cubits and a span (more than nine feet) tall and was well armed, carrying a large spear with an iron point that weighed 600 shekels (15 pounds), a javelin, and a sword. For protection, he wore a bronze helmet, a coat of bronze "scale" armor that weighed 5,000 shekels (125 pounds. Some translations say 6,000 shekels), and bronze "greaves" to protect his legs. His servant carried his shield.

✏ 3. Read 1 Samuel 17:5. What does the use of the word *scale* in describing Goliath's armor indicate?

Suggested Responses: It is a description befitting a snake, which symbolized the devil who tempted Adam and Eve in the Garden of Eden. It helps to communicate the evil that Goliath represented.

✏ 4. Who, in effect, did Goliath defy when he made his loud challenges? (See 1 Samuel 17:10.)

Suggested Response: Goliath defied the God of the Israelites as well as the Israelite people.

✏ 5. What, in David's mind, was really at stake in the contest between him and Goliath? (See 1 Samuel 17:26, 45.)

Suggested Response: David, who understood that Goliath was defying the "armies of the living God," recognized that the battle was a spiritual battle—a battle between God and Satan.

CULTURES IN CONTRAST

Israelites	Philistines
Lived mainly in mountainous areas	Lived on the fertile coastal plain
Had primitive technology	Had advanced iron technology
Worshiped the one true God	Worshiped many gods through extremely immoral religious practices, including sacred prostitution

small group bible discovery

Topic A: A Clash of Cultures

The battle in the Elah Valley is significant not because David, a young shepherd who was untrained in warfare, defeated Goliath, a giant of a warrior, but because of what the battle represented.

1. Read 1 Samuel 17:1–3 and answer the following questions.

   a. Describe how the two armies positioned themselves for battle in the Shephelah region.

   b. Which army was the aggressor?

   c. Why was this an important battle for both sides?

2. Read 1 Samuel 17:4–7, 51 and describe the kind of warrior Goliath was.

3. Read 1 Samuel 17:5. What does the use of the word *scale* in describing Goliath's armor indicate?

4. Who, in effect, did Goliath defy when he made his loud challenges? (See 1 Samuel 17:10.)

5. What, in David's mind, was really at stake in the contest between him and Goliath? (See 1 Samuel 17:26, 45.)

CULTURES IN CONTRAST

Israelites	Philistines
Lived mainly in mountainous areas	Lived on the fertile coastal plain
Had primitive technology	Had advanced iron technology
Worshiped the one true God	Worshiped many gods through extremely immoral religious practices, including sacred prostitution

PLANNING NOTES:

Topic B: The Battle Between God and Satan

Since the encounter in the Garden of Eden, the battle between God and Satan has been played out many times over in human history. Note the ways in which the writers of Scripture reveal their understanding of this battle through the events they record.

1. Read Genesis 3:14–15 and answer the following questions.

   a. What did God say would happen concerning the relationship between human beings and the devil and his seed?

   Suggested Response: There would be an ongoing battle between the off-spring of Eve and the offspring of Satan.

   b. How would Satan's descendants be destroyed?

   Suggested Response: The offspring of Eve would "crush" his head.

2. What is the parallel between Genesis 3:14–15 and the way in which Goliath died? (Read 1 Samuel 17:48–49.)

   Suggested Response: God promised that the offspring of Eve would crush Satan's head, and the rock slung by David—Eve's offspring and the servant of God—crushed the head of Goliath, Satan's representative.

3. Read Daniel 3:1 and answer the following questions.

   a. How tall and wide was the statue in cubits?

   Suggested Response: The statue was sixty cubits (ninety feet) tall and six cubits (nine feet) wide.

   b. What do the numbers the writer used reveal about the true nature of this image?

   Suggested Response: The image, described by multiples of the number six, represented Satan.

   c. Compare the height of Goliath in cubits (1 Samuel 17:4) with the dimensions of this statue. What does this reveal about Goliath's relationship to Satan?

   Suggested Response: Goliath was described by the number six, so he also represented Satan.

4. Compare what God said in Deuteronomy 17:14–17 with 2 Chronicles 9:13, 15, 18, 25–28. What is the writer revealing about the moral quality of Solomon's wealth?

   Suggested Responses: Through phrases such as "666 talents" of gold, shields made of "six hundred bekas" of gold, and "throne had six steps," the writer may be indicating that Solomon's wealth was not obtained according to God's standards. This wealth led toward evil rather than toward godliness.

Topic B: The Battle Between God and Satan

Since the encounter in the Garden of Eden, the battle between God and Satan has been played out many times over in human history. Note the ways in which the writers of Scripture reveal their understanding of this battle through the events they record.

1. Read Genesis 3:14–15 and answer the following questions.

   a. What did God say would happen concerning the relationship between human beings and the devil and his seed?

   b. How would Satan's descendants be destroyed?

2. What is the parallel between Genesis 3:14–15 and the way in which Goliath died? (Read 1 Samuel 17:48–49.)

3. Read Daniel 3:1 and answer the following questions.

   a. How tall and wide was the statue in cubits?

   b. What do the numbers the writer used reveal about the true nature of this image?

   c. Compare the height of Goliath in cubits (1 Samuel 17:4) with the dimensions of this statue. What does this reveal about Goliath's relationship to Satan?

4. Compare what God said in Deuteronomy 17:14–17 with 2 Chronicles 9:13, 15, 18, 25–28. What is the writer revealing about the moral quality of Solomon's wealth?

FACT FILE

Goliath

Philistine Armor

- Was a hardened warrior.
- Was more than nine feet tall.
- Wore a coat of bronze "scale" armor weighing 125 pounds. (The coat of mail was designed to protect its wearer without restricting movement.)
- Carried a spear that had a fifteen-pound point.
- Came from the Philistine city of Gath.
- Wore a bronze javelin on his back.
- Wore a bronze helmet.
- Defied the God of Israel ... and paid for it with his life.
- Symbolized evil, according to some scholars, who point to the ways in which the number six was used to describe him.

FACT FILE   **Philistine Armor**

Goliath

- Was a hardened warrior.
- Was more than nine feet tall.
- Wore a coat of bronze "scale" armor weighing 125 pounds. (The coat of mail was designed to protect its wearer without restricting movement.)
- Carried a spear that had a fifteen-pound point.
- Came from the Philistine city of Gath.
- Wore a bronze javelin on his back.
- Wore a bronze helmet.
- Defied the God of Israel . . . and paid for it with his life.
- Symbolized evil, according to some scholars, who point to the ways in which the number six was used to describe him.

Topic C: The Battle Is Won

1. As the Israelite and Philistine armies faced one another in the Elah Valley, the great disparity in the quality of their military equipment was evident. Read the following references and compare the equipment of each.

	Philistines	Israelites	David
1 Samuel 13:19, 22		2 swords, 2 spears	
1 Samuel 17:4–7	bronze helmets, armor, and greaves; bronze javelins, iron-tipped spears, and swords, shields		
1 Samuel 17:38–40		bronze helmet, armor (at least for Saul and Jonathan, but probably no one else)	wooden staff, five stones, a sling

Note: In addition to these weapons, there were archers on both sides. The Hebrew archers had arrows about eighteen inches long that could travel fifty to seventy feet. Although they are not mentioned in reference to this battle, the Philistines had iron chariots and could have used them in the wide Elah Valley.

88   Faith Lessons on the Promised Land

c. Compare the height of Goliath in cubits (1 Samuel 17:4) with the dimensions of this statue. What does this reveal about Goliath's relationship to Satan?

4. Compare what God said in Deuteronomy 17:14–17 with 2 Chronicles 9:13, 15, 18, 25–28. What is the writer revealing about the moral quality of Solomon's wealth?

FACT FILE

Goliath

Philistine Armor

- Was a hardened warrior.
- Was more than nine feet tall.
- Wore a coat of bronze "scale" armor weighing 125 pounds. (The coat of mail was designed to protect its wearer without restricting movement.)
- Carried a spear that had a fifteen-pound point.
- Came from the Philistine city of Gath.
- Wore a bronze javelin on his back.
- Wore a bronze helmet.
- Defied the God of Israel...and paid for it with his life.
- Symbolized evil, according to some scholars, who point to the ways in which the number six was used to describe him.

Session Five: Iron of Culture   89

Topic C: The Battle Is Won

As the Israelite and Philistine armies faced one another in the Elah Valley, the great disparity in the quality of their military equipment was evident. Read the following references and compare the equipment of each.

	Philistines	Israelites	David
1 Samuel 13:19, 22			
1 Samuel 17:4–7			
1 Samuel 17:38–40			

2. What is significant about the way in which David approached the battle? (Read 1 Samuel 17:45–47.)

EVIDENCE FILE

Discoveries About Philistine Warriors

After finding carvings of Philistine soldiers in the temple of Ramses III in Egypt, archaeologists discovered that the soldiers:

- Wore feathered helmets secured under their chins by leather straps. Headbands, probably of metal, held the feathers in place.
- Wore breastplates and short skirts that had wide hems and tassels.
- Were clean shaven and quite tall.
- Sometimes carried small, round shields and straight swords.

SPOTLIGHT ON THE EVIDENCE

Discoveries About Philistine Warriors

After finding carvings of Philistine soldiers in the temple of Ramses III in Egypt, archaeologists discovered that the soldiers:

- Wore feathered helmets secured under their chins by leather straps. Head-bands, probably of metal, held the feathers in place.
- Wore breastplates and short skirts that had wide hems and tassels.
- Were clean shaven and quite tall.
- Sometimes carried small, round shields and straight swords.

 2. What is significant about the way in which David approached the battle? (Read 1 Samuel 17:45–47.)

Suggested Responses: He considered it to be God's battle, not his own; he came in the name of the Lord to give glory to the living God of Israel; he had confidence that God would make Israel victorious; etc.

 3. God chose David and used his skill with the sling to gain victory. What does this demonstrate about the way in which God uses people—even their most simple talents—to accomplish His purposes?

Suggested Response: Just as God used David, a young shepherd armed with a sling, to gain victory over the Philistines, He can use our simple talents to accomplish His purposes.

Tel Azekah

Topic C: The Battle Is Won

As the Israelite and Philistine armies faced one another in the Elah Valley, the great disparity in the quality of their military equipment was evident. Read the following references and compare the equipment of each.

	Philistines	Israelites	David
1 Samuel 13:19, 22			
1 Samuel 17:4–7			
1 Samuel 17:38–40			

2. What is significant about the way in which David approached the battle? (Read 1 Samuel 17:45–47.)

EVIDENCE FILE

Discoveries About Philistine Warriors

After finding carvings of Philistine soldiers in the temple of Ramses III in Egypt, archaeologists discovered that the soldiers:

- Wore feathered helmets secured under their chins by leather straps. Headbands, probably of metal, held the feathers in place.
- Wore breastplates and short skirts that had wide hems and tassels.
- Were clean shaven and quite tall.
- Sometimes carried small, round shields and straight swords.

---

3. God chose David and used his skill with the sling to gain victory. What does this demonstrate about the way in which God uses people—even their most simple talents—to accomplish His purposes?

4. Describe how each side responded to David's victory (1 Samuel 17:51–53).

   a. The Philistines:

   b. The Israelites:

Tel Azekah

✏ 4. Describe how each side responded to David's victory (See 1 Samuel 17:51–53).

    a. The Philistines:

    Suggested Responses: They became afraid, abandoned their camp, and ran home to their cities. Many of the Philistines were killed on the way.

    b. The Israelites:

    Suggested Responses: The Israelite soldiers surged forward with a shout and chased the fleeing Philistines all the way to their cities on the coastal plain. Then they plundered the Philistines' camp on their return home.

Topic D: The Consequences of Disobedience—Saul's Failure to Fulfill God's Calling

✏ 1. How did King Saul respond to David's continued success in fighting the Philistines? (Read 1 Samuel 18:5–9, 12–16, 20–21, 24–25.)

Suggested Responses: King Saul initially gave David a high rank in the army, which pleased the people and Saul's officers. But Saul became angry, jealous, and afraid of David because the young man was so loved and successful. So Saul schemed to use the promise of marriage to one of his daughters as a way to have David killed by the Philistines.

✏ 2. Early in the Israelites' history, what did God command the Israelites to do? (Read Deuteronomy 25:17–19.)

Suggested Response: To kill all the Amalekites.

✏ 3. Years later, whom did God choose to destroy the Amalekites? (Read 1 Samuel 15:1–3.)

Suggested Response: Saul.

✏ 4. What did Saul do to the Amalekites? (Read 1 Samuel 15:7–10.)

Suggested Responses: He destroyed the Amalekite people but disobeyed God by allowing King Agag and the best animals to live.

✏ 5. About 400 years later, what did Haman—a descendant of Agag—plan to do to all the Jews? (Read Esther 3:1–11.) If Haman had done this, what would have happened to God's plan of salvation?

Suggested Responses: Haman received permission from King Xerxes to destroy all the Jews and even agreed to pay the murderers for the deed. If this had occurred, God's plan of salvation through Jesus would have been thwarted.

✏ 6. What is significant about Esther's family heritage, and how did God use her to save the Jews? (Read 1 Samuel 9:1–2; Esther 2:5–7, 17; 6:1–10; 7:1–7, 9; 9:5–10.)

Suggested Responses: Esther—who became the queen of King Xerxes—was a descendant of Kish, Saul's father. After King Xerxes learned how Esther's cousin, Mordecai, had saved his life, Esther was faithful to God and petitioned the king

Topic D: The Consequences of Disobedience—Saul's Failure to Fulfill God's Calling

1. How did King Saul respond to David's continued success in fighting the Philistines? (Read 1 Samuel 18:5–9, 12–16, 20–21, 24–25.)

2. Early in the Israelites' history, what did God command the Israelites to do? (Read Deuteronomy 25:17–19.)

3. Years later, whom did God choose to destroy the Amalekites? (Read 1 Samuel 15:1–3.)

4. What did Saul do to the Amalekites? (Read 1 Samuel 15:7–10.)

5. About 400 years later, what did Haman—a descendant of Agag—plan to do to all the Jews? (Read Esther 3:1–11.) If Haman had done this, what would have happened to God's plan of salvation?

6. What is significant about Esther's family heritage, and how did God use her to save the Jews? (Read 1 Samuel 9:1–2; Esther 2:5–7, 17; 6:1–10; 7:1–7, 9; 9:5–10.)

Topic E: Choosing God's Ways or the World's Ways

Solomon was the wisest king who ever lived. Yet in many ways he failed to obey God. In so doing, he allowed the world's culture to shape him rather than using his gifts to influence the culture for God.

1. God provided clear instructions for those who would be king over His people. Compare the following commands with Solomon's response.

God's Command	Solomon's Response
Deuteronomy 17:16:	2 Chronicles 9:25, 28:
Deuteronomy 17:17a:	1 Kings 11:1–3:
Deuteronomy 17:17b:	2 Chronicles 9:13–14, 27:

2. The wisest human king who ever lived failed to obey God and thus fell short of his calling. But there is another king who described himself as "one greater than Solomon."

    a. Who is He? (See Matthew 12:42.)

PLANNING NOTES:

to save the Jews from Haman's scheme. The king agreed and executed Haman, and the Jews later killed Haman's sons. So, God gave the family of Saul an opportunity to be faithful and preserve God's plan from the tragedy Saul had created by not killing King Agag.

Topic E: Choosing God's Ways or the World's Ways

Solomon was the wisest king who ever lived. Yet in many ways he failed to obey God. In so doing, he allowed the world's culture to shape him rather than using his gifts to influence the culture for God.

✎ 1. God provided clear instructions for those who would be king over His people. Compare the following commands with Solomon's response.

God's Command	Solomon's Response
Deuteronomy 17:16: Don't acquire great numbers of horses or send people to Egypt to get them	2 Chronicles 9:25, 28: had 4,000 stalls for horses and chariots, 12,000 horses, and imported horses from Egypt
Deuteronomy 17:17a: Don't take many wives because they will lead your heart astray	1 Kings 11:1–3: loved many foreign women—had 700 wives and 300 concubines, who led him astray
Deuteronomy 17:17b: Don't accumulate large amounts of silver and gold	2 Chronicles 9:13–14, 27: received "666" talents of gold annually plus revenues from trading, plus gold and silver from kings and governors; made silver as common as stones in

✎ 2. The wisest human king who ever lived failed to obey God and thus fell short of his calling. But there is another king who described himself as "one greater than Solomon."

a. Who is He? (See Matthew 12:42.)

Suggested Response: Jesus.

b. What is His all-consuming purpose? (See Matthew 18:11; Luke 22:39–42; John 4:34; 14:8–13; 1 Timothy 2:5–6.)

Suggested Responses: to do the will of God, to reveal God, to redeem the human race.

6. What is significant about Esther's family heritage, and how did God use her to save the Jews? (Read 1 Samuel 9:1–2; Esther 2:5–7, 17; 6:1–10; 7:1–7, 9; 9:5–10.)

Topic E: Choosing God's Ways or the World's Ways

Solomon was the wisest king who ever lived. Yet in many ways he failed to obey God. In so doing, he allowed the world's culture to shape him rather than using his gifts to influence the culture for God.

1. God provided clear instructions for those who would be king over His people. Compare the following commands with Solomon's response.

God's Command	Solomon's Response
Deuteronomy 17:16:	2 Chronicles 9:25, 28:
Deuteronomy 17:17a:	1 Kings 11:1–3:
Deuteronomy 17:17b:	2 Chronicles 9:13–14, 27:

2. The wisest human king who ever lived failed to obey God and thus fell short of his calling. But there is another king who described himself as "one greater than Solomon."

    a. Who is He? (See Matthew 12:42.)

b. What is His all-consuming purpose? (See Matthew 18:11; Luke 22:39–42; John 4:34; 14:8–13; 1 Timothy 2:5–6.)

faith Lesson

Time for Reflection

Please read the following passage of Scripture silently and take the next few minutes to reflect on what the battle between David and Goliath was all about.

Goliath stood and shouted,... "This day I defy the ranks of Israel! Give me a man and let us fight each other." On hearing the Philistine's words, Saul and all the Israelites were dismayed and terrified....

David said to Saul, "Let no one lose heart on account of this Philistine; your servant will go and fight him."

Saul replied, "You are not able to go out against this Philistine and fight him; you are only a boy, and he has been a fighting man from his youth."

But David said to Saul, "Your servant has been keeping his father's sheep. When a lion or a bear came and carried off a sheep from the flock, I went after it, struck it and rescued the sheep from its mouth. When it turned on me, I seized it by its hair, struck it and killed it. Your servant has killed both the lion and the bear; this uncircumcised Philistine will be like one of them, because he has defied the armies of the living God. The Lord who delivered me from the paw of the lion and the paw of the bear will deliver me from the hand of this Philistine." ...

David said to the Philistine, "You come against me with sword and spear and javelin, but I come against you in the name of the Lord Almighty, the God of the armies of Israel, whom you have defied. This day the Lord will hand you over to me, and I'll strike you down

faith Lesson

Time for Reflection (5 minutes)

It's time for each of us to think quietly about how we can apply what we've learned today. On page 93 of the Participant's Guide, you'll find a passage of Scripture. Let's each read this passage silently and take the next few minutes to consider some of the questions that follow.

Please do not talk during this time. It's a time when we all can reflect on today's lesson and how it applies to our lives.

> *The Scripture passage and questions are reproduced in their entirety in the Participant's Guide on pages 93–94.*

Goliath stood and shouted, . . . "This day I defy the ranks of Israel! Give me a man and let us fight each other." On hearing the Philistine's words, Saul and all the Israelites were dismayed and terrified. . . .

David said to Saul, "Let no one lose heart on account of this Philistine; your servant will go and fight him."

Saul replied, "You are not able to go out against this Philistine and fight him; you are only a boy, and he has been a fighting man from his youth."

But David said to Saul, "Your servant has been keeping his father's sheep. When a lion or a bear came and carried off a sheep from the flock, I went after it, struck it and rescued the sheep from its mouth. When it turned on me, I seized it by its hair, struck it and killed it. Your servant has killed both the lion and the bear; this uncircumcised Philistine will be like one of them, because he has defied the armies of the living God. The LORD who delivered me from the paw of the lion and the paw of the bear will deliver me from the hand of this Philistine." . . .

David said to the Philistine, "You come against me with sword and spear and javelin, but I come against you in the name of the LORD Almighty, the God of the armies of Israel, whom you have defied. This day the LORD will hand you over to me, and I'll strike you down and cut off your head. Today I will give the carcasses of the Philistine army to the birds of the air and the beasts of the earth, and the whole world will know that there is a God in Israel. All those gathered here will know that it is not by sword or spear that the LORD saves; for the battle is the LORD's, and he will give all of you into our hands."

1 SAMUEL 17:8, 10–11, 32–37, 45–47

1. How do the motives David had in challenging Goliath (17:45–46) apply to Christians today who are called to challenge the evils of our culture?

2. David recognized that the battle with Goliath was God's battle, not his battle. How does that belief empower you to use your gifts and talents to confront evil in your culture?

b. What is His all-consuming purpose? (See Matthew 18:11; Luke 22:39–42; John 4:34; 14:8–13; 1 Timothy 2:5–6.)

faith Lesson

Time for Reflection

Please read the following passage of Scripture silently and take the next few minutes to reflect on what the battle between David and Goliath was all about.

> Goliath stood and shouted, . . . "This day I defy the ranks of Israel! Give me a man and let us fight each other." On hearing the Philistine's words, Saul and all the Israelites were dismayed and terrified. . . .
>
> David said to Saul, "Let no one lose heart on account of this Philistine; your servant will go and fight him."
>
> Saul replied, "You are not able to go out against this Philistine and fight him; you are only a boy, and he has been a fighting man from his youth."
>
> But David said to Saul, "Your servant has been keeping his father's sheep. When a lion or a bear came and carried off a sheep from the flock, I went after it, struck it and rescued the sheep from its mouth. When it turned on me, I seized it by its hair, struck it and killed it. Your servant has killed both the lion and the bear; this uncircumcised Philistine will be like one of them, because he has defied the armies of the living God. The LORD who delivered me from the paw of the lion and the paw of the bear will deliver me from the hand of this Philistine." . . .
>
> David said to the Philistine, "You come against me with sword and spear and javelin, but I come against you in the name of the LORD Almighty, the God of the armies of Israel, whom you have defied. This day the LORD will hand you over to me, and I'll strike you down

> and cut off your head. Today I will give the carcasses of the Philistine army to the birds of the air and the beasts of the earth, and the whole world will know that there is a God in Israel. All those gathered here will know that it is not by sword or spear that the LORD saves; for the battle is the LORD's, and he will give all of you into our hands."

1 SAMUEL 17:8, 10–11, 32–37, 45–47

1. How do the motives David had in challenging Goliath (17:45–46) apply to Christians today who are called to challenge the evils of our culture?

2. David recognized that the battle with Goliath was God's battle, not his battle. How does that belief empower you to use your gifts and talents to confront evil in your culture?

3. When David stepped out in faith and used his skills for God, the Israelite soldiers regained confidence in themselves and God and won a great victory. How might you encourage and influence your family or friends for God by stepping out in faith to promote God and His values? Think of a situation in which you could stand up for the Lord and encourage other people.

4. When David killed Goliath, the Philistine soldiers saw the power of God at work and ran away. How might people respond to you when you step forward in faith and use your skills and talents in God's service?

PLANNING NOTES:

✏ 3. When David stepped out in faith and used his skills for God, the Israelite soldiers regained confidence in themselves and God and won a great victory. How might you encourage and influence your family or friends for God by stepping out in faith to promote God and His values? Think of a situation in which you could stand up for the Lord and encourage other people.

✏ 4. When David killed Goliath, the Philistine soldiers saw the power of God at work and ran away. How might people respond to you when you step forward in faith and use your skills and talents in God's service?

> As soon as participants have spent five minutes reflecting on the above questions, get the entire group's attention and move to the next section.

Action Points (3 minutes)

> The following points are reproduced on pages 95–96 of the Participant's Guide:

Now it's time to wrap up our session.

> Give participants a moment to transition from their thoughtfulness to giving you their full attention.

I'd like to take a moment to summarize the key points we explored. After I have reviewed these points, I will give you a moment to jot down an action step (or steps) that you will commit to do this week as a result of what you have learned today.

> Read the following points and pause after each point so that participants can consider and write out their commitment.

✏ 1. *God can use people who seem to have little to offer to accomplish His purposes.* When we seek to accomplish God's work, our motivation and faith in God is far more significant than our talent or resources. David, for example, was a young shepherd who appeared to have little to offer, but he acted as God's representative. He used his training and primitive tools in order to reveal the God of Israel to the world of his day. He used a simple sling to throw a stone at a man who had the best military technology an advanced culture could offer—and he triumphed because God honored his throw.

Which gifts or talents, no matter how insignificant they may seem from a human viewpoint, are you willing to use to accomplish God's work?

✏ 2. *God wants each of us to use our particular gifts and talents to influence our culture for Him.* David did what God had qualified and gifted him to do, and because David was motivated by righteousness, he made a powerful impact on his culture. Likewise, we don't have to be anything other than the people

and cut off your head. Today I will give the carcasses of the Philistine army to the birds of the air and the beasts of the earth, and the whole world will know that there is a God in Israel. All those gathered here will know that it is not by sword or spear that the LORD saves; for the battle is the LORD's, and he will give all of you into our hands."

1 SAMUEL 17:8, 10–11, 32–37, 45–47

1. How do the motives David had in challenging Goliath (17:45–46) apply to Christians today who are called to challenge the evils of our culture?

2. David recognized that the battle with Goliath was God's battle, not his battle. How does that belief empower you to use your gifts and talents to confront evil in your culture?

3. When David stepped out in faith and used his skills for God, the Israelite soldiers regained confidence in themselves and God and won a great victory. How might you encourage and influence your family or friends for God by stepping out in faith to promote God and His values? Think of a situation in which you could stand up for the Lord and encourage other people.

4. When David killed Goliath, the Philistine soldiers saw the power of God at work and ran away. How might people respond to you when you step forward in faith and use your skills and talents in God's service?

Action Points

Please take the next few moments to review the lessons of the battle between David and Goliath. Consider how those lessons apply to your life and make a commitment to take action because of what you have learned.

1. *God can use people who seem to have little to offer to accomplish His purposes.* When we seek to accomplish God's work, our motivation and faith in God is far more significant than our talent or resources. David, for example, was a young shepherd who appeared to have little to offer, but he acted as God's representative. He used his training and primitive tools in order to reveal the God of Israel to the world of his day. He used a simple sling to throw a stone at a man who had the best military technology an advanced culture could offer—and he triumphed because God honored his throw.

   Which gifts or talents, no matter how insignificant they may seem from a human viewpoint, are you willing to use to accomplish God's work?

2. *God wants each of us to use our particular gifts and talents to influence our culture for Him.*

   David did what God had qualified and gifted him to do, and because David was motivated by righteousness, he made a powerful impact on his culture. Likewise, we don't have to be anything other than the people God has created us to be in order to accomplish His purposes. Who He has made us to be is good enough. We need only to express the gifts and talents He has given us.

PLANNING NOTES:

God has created us to be in order to accomplish His purposes. Who He has made us to be is good enough. We need only to express the gifts and talents He has given us.

In what way(s) can you use your gifts and talents to honor God and influence the culture around you? Be specific.

✏ 3. *God wants us to use every resource, including the tools and technology of our culture—its "iron"—to accomplish His purposes.* The Israelites achieved a decisive victory over the Philistines when David killed Goliath. Unfortunately, the Philistines remained the superior culture for quite a while afterward (1 Samuel 31). Only when the Israelites, under the reign of faithful King David, harnessed the Philistines' advanced iron technology and used it for God's purposes did they become a great influence and power. Today, Christians who hold a Bible-based value system and are able to shape and control the "iron" aspects of their society will greatly impact their culture.

Which technologies that are shaping the culture of our society—its "iron," so to speak—can you impact for God while remaining faithful to the standards He has set for you? (The field of law? Politics? Education? Journalism? Movie production? Community?)

How could you support others who help shape the iron of our culture?

closing prayer
I minute

Dear God, thank You for Your faithfulness to us, for standing beside us in our daily lives. How easy it is to stand on the sidelines instead of standing for You and getting involved in the spiritual battle. Please give us the strength to stand up for You. Help us to use our gifts and talents to harness the iron of our culture and use it to promote and glorify You. Amen.

In what way(s) can you use your gifts and talents to honor God and influence the culture around you? Be specific.

3. *God wants us to use every resource, including the tools and technology of our culture—its "iron"—to accomplish His purposes.* The Israelites achieved a decisive victory over the Philistines when David killed Goliath. Unfortunately, the Philistines remained the superior culture for quite a while afterward (1 Samuel 31). Only when the Israelites, under the reign of faithful King David, harnessed the Philistines' advanced iron technology and used it for God's purposes did they become a great influence and power. Today, Christians who hold a Bible-based value system and are able to shape and control the "iron" aspects of their society will greatly impact their culture.

Which technologies that are shaping the culture of our society—its "iron," so to speak—can you impact for God while remaining faithful to the standards He has set for you? (The field of law? Politics? Education? Journalism? Movie production? Community?)

How could you support others who help shape the iron of our culture?

PLANNING NOTES:

additional resources

History

Connolly, Peter. *Living in the Time of Jesus of Nazareth.* Tel Aviv: Steimatzky, 1983.

Ward, Kaari. *Jesus and His Times.* New York: Reader's Digest, 1987.

Whiston, William, trans. *The Works of Josephus: Complete and Unabridged.* Peabody, Mass.: Hendrikson Publishers, 1987.

Wood, Leon. Revised by David O'Brien. *A Survey of Israel's History.* Grand Rapids: Zondervan, 1986.

Jewish Roots of Christianity

Stern, David H. *Jewish New Testament Commentary.* Clarksville, Md.: Jewish New Testament Publications, 1992.

Wilson, Marvin R. *Our Father Abraham: Jewish Roots of the Christian Faith.* Grand Rapids: Eerdmans, 1986.

Young, Brad H. *Jesus the Jewish Theologian.* Peabody, Mass.: Hendrickson Publishers, 1995.

Geography

Beitzel, Barry J. *The Moody Atlas of Bible Lands.* Chicago: Moody Press, 1993.

Gardner, Joseph L. *Reader's Digest Atlas of the Bible.* New York: Reader's Digest, 1993.

General Background

Alexander, David, and Pat Alexander, eds. *Eerdmans' Handbook to the Bible.* Grand Rapids: Eerdmans, 1983.

Butler, Trent C., ed. *Holman Bible Dictionary.* Nashville: Holman Bible Publishers, 1991.

Edersheim, Alfred. *The Life and Times of Jesus the Messiah.* Peabody, Mass.: Hendrickson Publishers, 1994.

Archaeological Background

Charlesworth, James H. *Jesus Within Judaism: New Light from Exciting Archaeological Discoveries.* New York: Doubleday, 1988.

Finegan, Jack. *The Archaeology of the New Testament: The Life of Jesus and the Beginning of the Early Church.* Princeton: Princeton University Press, 1978.

Mazar, Amihai. *Archaeology of the Land of the Bible: 10,000–586 B.C.E.* New York: Doubleday, 1990.

To learn more about the specific backgrounds of this set of videos, consult the following resources:

Avigad, Nahman. "Jerusalem in Flames—The Burnt House Captures a Moment in Time." *Biblical Archaeology Review* (November-December 1983).

Barkey, Gabriel. "The Garden Tomb—Was Jesus Buried Here?" *Biblical Archaeology Review* (March-April 1986).

Ben Dov, Meir. "Herod's Mighty Temple Mount." *Biblical Archaeology Review* (November-December 1986).

Bivin, David. "The Miraculous Catch." *Jerusalem Perspective* (March-April 1992).

Burrell, Barbara, Kathryn Gleason, and Ehud Netzer. "Uncovering Herod's Seaside Palace." *Biblical Archaeology Review* (May-June 1993).

Edersheim, Alfred. *The Temple.* London: James Clarke & Co., 1959.

Edwards, William D., Wesley J. Gabel, and Floyd E. Hosmer. "On the Physical Death of Jesus Christ." *Journal of American Medical Association (JAMA)* (March 21, 1986).

Flusser, David. "To Bury Caiaphas, Not to Praise Him." *Jerusalem Perspective* (July-October 1991).

Greenhut, Zvi. "Burial Cave of the Caiaphas Family." *Biblical Archaeology Review* (September-October 1992).

Hareuveni, Nogah. *Nature in Our Biblical Heritage.* Kiryat Ono, Israel: Neot Kedumim, Ltd., 1980.

Hepper, F. Nigel. *Baker Encyclopedia of Bible Plants: Flowers and Trees, Fruits and Vegetables, Ecology.* Ed. by J. Gordon Melton. Grand Rapids: Baker, 1993.

"The 'High Priest' of the Jewish Quarter." *Biblical Archaeology Review* (May-June 1992).

Hirschfeld, Yizhar, and Giora Solar. "Sumptuous Roman Baths Uncovered Near Sea of Galilee." *Biblical Archaeology Review* (November-December 1984).

Hohlfelder, Robert L. "Caesarea Maritima: Herod the Great's City on the Sea." *National Geographic* (February 1987).

Holum, Kenneth G. *King Herod's Dream: Caesarea on the Sea.* New York: W. W. Norton, 1988.

Mazar, Benjamin. "Excavations Near Temple Mount Reveal Splendors of Herodian Jerusalem." *Biblical Archaeology Review* (July-August 1980).

Nun, Mendel. *Ancient Stone Anchors and Net Sinkers from the Sea of Galilee.* Israel: Kibbutz Ein Gev, 1993. (Also available from *Jerusalem Perspective*.)

_____. "Fish, Storms, and a Boat." *Jerusalem Perspective* (March-April 1990).

_____. "The Kingdom of Heaven Is Like a Seine." *Jerusalem Perspective* (November-December 1989).

_____. "Net Upon the Waters: Fish and Fishermen in Jesus' Time." *Biblical Archaeology Review* (November-December 1993).

_____. *The Sea of Galilee and Its Fishermen in the New Testament.* Israel: Kibbutz Ein Gev, 1993. (Also available from *Jerusalem Perspective*.)

Pileggi, David. "A Life on the Kinneret." *Jerusalem Perspective* (November-December 1989).

Pixner, Bargil. *With Jesus Through Galilee According to the Fifth Gospel.* Rosh Pina, Israel: Corazin Publishing, 1992.

Pope, Marvin, H. "Hosanna: What It Really Means." *Bible Review* (April 1988).

Riech, Ronny. "Ossuary Inscriptions from the Caiaphas Tomb." *Jerusalem Perspective* (July-October 1991).

_____. "Six Stone Water Jars." *Jerusalem Perspective* (July-September 1995).

Ritmeyer, Kathleen. "A Pilgrim's Journey." *Biblical Archaeology Review* (November-December 1989).

Ritmeyer, Kathleen, and Leen Ritmeyer. "Reconstructing Herod's Temple Mount in Jerusalem." *Biblical Archaeology Review* (November-December 1989).

_____. "Reconstructing the Triple Gate." *Biblical Archaeology Review* (November-December 1989).

transform your life through a journey of discovery into the world of the Bible
Faith Lessons Video Series
Ray Vander Laan

Filmed on location in Israel, Faith Lessons is a unique video series that brings God's Word to life with astounding relevance. By weaving together the Bible's fascinating historical, cultural, religious, and geographical contexts, teacher and historian Ray Vander Laan reveals keen insights into Scripture's significance for modern believers.

"Nothing has opened and illuminated the Scriptures for me quite like the Faith Lessons series."
—Dr. James Dobson

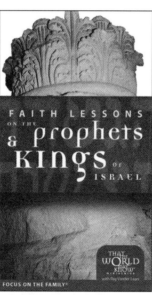

Faith Lessons on the Promised Land
Crossroads of the World
Volume One
 0-310-67864-1

Faith Lessons on the Prophets & Kings of Israel
Volume Two
0-310-67865-X

Faith Lessons on the Life & Ministry of the Messiah
Volume Three
0-310-67866-8

Faith Lessons on the Death & Resurrection of the Messiah
Volume Four
0-310-67867-6

also available:

*Jesus
An Interactive Journey*
CD-ROM
0-310-67888-9

Echoes of His Presence
Ray Vander Laan
Hardcover 0-310-67886-2
Audio 0-310-67887-0